1970

DEVOTIONAL POETS OF
THE SEVENTEENTH CENTURY

DEVOTIONAL POETS
of the Seventeenth Century

Edited by
SIR HENRY NEWBOLT

THOMAS NELSON AND SONS LTD
LONDON EDINBURGH PARIS MELBOURNE
TORONTO AND NEW YORK

THOMAS NELSON AND SONS LTD
Parkside Works Edinburgh 9
36 Park Street London W1
312 Flinders Street Melbourne C1

302–304 Barclays Bank Building
Commissioner and Kruis Streets
Johannesburg

THOMAS NELSON AND SONS (CANADA) LTD
91–93 Wellington Street West   Toronto 1

THOMAS NELSON AND SONS
19 East 47th Street New York 17

SOCIÉTÉ FRANÇAISE D'EDITIONS NELSON
25 rue Henri Barbusse Paris V^e

CONTENTS

RICHARD CRASHAW

ROBERT HERRICK
NOBLE NUMBERS

Contents

vii

Contents

Contents

HENRY VAUGHAN

THOMAS TRAHERNE

INTRODUCTION

by

SIR HENRY NEWBOLT

THE inferiority of most religious verse is not difficult to explain : it is due to the introduction of extraneous matter into the works of art. In poetry, as in painting, the creative imagination takes its material from this world, the world of Time, and recreates it by a process not only of construction but of transfiguration : we see our own life, but we see it made new for us, and glowing under a light which transcends the beauty of the actual world and has an imperishable quality otherwhere unknown. But when the creative emotion which drives the artist to write or paint happens to be a religious one, he too often falls into the mistake of advocating or illustrating—that is, of adding something which is not his own : he includes in the fabric of his new world a number of details or dogmas which are unsuitable material for any artistic purpose, either because they are argumentative or abstract, or historical or theoretical, or because they belong to a life of which we have at present no familiar or generally accepted knowledge. But if he will avoid this natural temptation it is possible for a painter to paint a good picture on a religious subject—he has only to show us the divine on earth and not in the sky—and it will even be possible for a poet to make good religious poetry : he has only to rely on his own religious experience, that which comes to him from no outward source, and yet is common to him and to an immense number of his human fellows.

Though this possibility is always with us, it has rarely brought us any but small and scattered gifts. We have had religious poems, but seldom devotional poets. From the seventeenth century alone have we received volumes of verse upon religious themes, so charged with sincere religious emotion as to be essentially independent of religious dogma. The six poets whose devotional work makes up our present collection are by no means all of the same rank, but they are all sincere, and though their allegiance was given to different schools of religious thought there is in their poetry little or nothing of a sectarian kind, in the controversial sense of the word. This common purity of temperament and the literary connection which exists between their work, makes it proper to consider them as a group, and even as a group characteristic of a particular century. We need not believe that human nature changes at every hundredth year and at no other time ; but we may and must recognize that both art and intellect have their clearly marked tides. The poetry, and especially the more serious poetry, produced between 1610, when Donne began to publish, and 1695, when Vaughan died, is clearly distinguished from the typical work of the Elizabethan age or of the eighteenth century. And this is exactly what we might expect, for the period was one of prolonged religious unrest. The social confusion, which had begun with the transition from the Roman to the Anglican system, was renewed by the schemes of the Stuarts and their supporters, and only ended by the bloodless violence of the Revolution of 1688. During these troubles an Englishman, on whatever side he might be, had to pay dearly for his faith : and the poets suffered at least as much as others. Yet only one of any stature mingled partisanship with his poetry : and we are relieved from the task of considering this one exception by the obvious fact that Milton, though in his own way intensely religious, does not fall within our proposed group—he is not the author of a body of devotional poetry.

The first poet in our collection, John Donne, was by

birth an Elizabethan and a Roman Catholic : that is to say, he was born in 1573 and his parents had lived through the clash of Reformation and Counter-Reformation without accepting the national decision. Their son was entered at Hart Hall, Oxford, in 1584, and at Lincoln's Inn in 1590. But either his spirit or his social opportunities soon led him away from a professional career. In 1595 he sailed with Essex in the expedition against Cadiz : in 1597 he made " the Islands Voyage " under the same commander. Then he became Secretary to Sir Thomas Egerton, the Lord Keeper, afterwards Lord Chancellor, and presumed so far as not only to fall in love with the great man's niece, Anne More, but to marry her clandestinely. For this crime, when discovered, he was imprisoned in the Fleet at the instance of his father-in-law, Sir George More, and upon his release he lived a precarious life in the employ of different masters, the last of whom was Dr. Morton, afterwards Bishop of Durham, and in the meantime engaged in controversy with the Roman Catholics. Donne's assistance was so much to his liking that he offered him immediate preferment if he would enter the Church of England. Donne refused, but only four years later he had gone far enough to publish a pasquinade against the Jesuits. Finally in 1614, after more patrons had disappointed him, he was practically commanded by James the First to take Anglican Orders. He was ordained in January 1615, and only six years afterwards was appointed Dean of St. Paul's, where he proved himself to be the greatest preacher as well as the greatest poet of his time. He lost his wife in 1617, and died himself in 1631.

George Herbert, who is sometimes said to have " followed " Donne, certainly resembles him in one particular quality — the so-called " metaphysical " quality of his poetry. Both may be said to have smelted the stone of the street for the gold of the Spirit : they sought Reality by realism. But their aims and methods were not the same. Donne spent his gigantic strength in trying to find that which seems to lie beyond discovery, to express that which was never yet expressed. Herbert, with a less chaotic experience, and less strength of every kind, came nearer to success within his own chosen limits. His aim is not so much to discover, as to exhibit in new ways what he has long known. He has no need to invent a new kind of verse : and his conceits are above all designed to be intelligible—they are examples chosen from familiar life but used with a dexterous twist which makes them attractive and memorable. But a greater difference lies beneath : the difference of natural temperament. Donne was a multiple man, self tortured and self torn. His violent repentance of his earlier loves and less divine poems was only one of many rebellions in his inner life. Herbert, though for a time he enjoyed Court favour and hesitated to take Orders, can never have suffered greatly—with perfect simplicity, perfect sincerity, and perfect fitness for his own place in the world he needed only the joy of expression, and that he perceived to be attainable by the most unlaboured method.

> " How wide is all this long pretence !
> There is in Love a sweetness ready penned :
> Copy out only that, and save expence."

Herbert's life, too, shows that he can hardly have been influenced by Donne's poems ; for most of them, and in particular the *Divine Poems*, were only published in 1633, when both poets were dead. Nor is there any record of friendship between them. Herbert was twenty years younger than Donne : he was at Cambridge, as undergraduate, fellow, and Public Orator, until after Donne had lost his wife and retired into the country, so that they cannot have met at Court ; and his last years were passed in the remote parsonage of Bemerton while Donne was practising a morbid and fantastic asceticism at St. Paul's.

Donne died in 1631, Herbert in 1632. The posthumous poems of both appeared in 1633. There were then living two boys who eventually shared the Herbert inheritance between them, but spent it to far different purpose: Richard Crashaw, then aged twenty, and Henry Vaughan, aged twelve. Crashaw was the son of a Protestant theologian, who sent him to Charterhouse and to Pembroke College, Cambridge. Richard, however, migrated to Peterhouse in 1636, and remained there till 1641, when " the troubles " began, and Strafford was executed. In 1644, when Parliament signed the Covenant, Crashaw refused, and joined the King's party at Oxford. After the destruction of the Royalist army at Naseby in 1645 he left the country, and in the following year was found in Paris by his friend Cowley and presented to the Queen. He was appointed a Canon of Loretto, having in the meantime read the works of St. Teresa and thereupon thrown himself into the arms of the Roman Church. It is probable that in that communion he found more appreciation than he would ever have gained from contemporary Anglicans; but that he was always sincere, from first to last the same ardent spirit, is clearly proved by at least two of his poems. One is the *Apology* for his *Hymn to the Name and Honour of the Admirable Saint Teresa*, " as having been writ when the Author was yet among the Protestants "; the other the exquisite little poem *On Mr. George Herbert's Book, entitled The Temple : Sent to a Gentlewoman*, in which he claims to be one with his Anglican master.

> " Know you, Fair, on what you look ?
> Divinest love is in this book . . .
> And though Herbert's name do owe
> These devotions : fairest, know
> While I thus lay them on the shrine
> Of your white hand, they are mine."

Unfortunately he had a taste in " conceits " which shows him—or one side of him—to be of a temperament

wholly alien from Herbert's. It is useless to complain
of a poet who is evidently himself; but when he has
claimed to be made in the likeness of another, it is dis-
appointing to find more caricature than resemblance.
The Herbertian element is very marked in Crashaw's
poem on *Saint Mary Magdalene, or The Weeper* : yet it
uses images with such crude and puerile absurdity as to
combine lack of reverence with lack of humour. When
the Magdalen weeps for her Lord we are told—

> " And now where'er He stays
> Among the Galilean mountains,
> Or more unwelcome ways ;
> He's followed by two faithful fountains ;
> Two walking baths, two weeping motions,
> Portable and compendious oceans."

It is incredible—this much we may say—that these
lines, and many more of the same frigid and turgid sort,
should have come from the man who wrote the Hymn
of the Shepherds, *In the Holy Nativity of Our Lord God*,
or the stanzas of the *Dies Iræ, Dies Illa*, which inspired
the music of Blake's most original lyric.

> " O that fire, before whose face
> Heaven and Earth shall find no place,
> O those eyes, whose angry light
> Must be the day of that dread night.

> *   *   *   *   *   *

> Dear, remember in that day
> Who was the cause Thou cam'st this way.
> Thy sheep was stray'd ; and Thou would'st be
> Even lost Thyself in seeking me.

> Shall all that labour, all that cost
> Of love, and even that loss, be lost ?
> And this loved soul, judged worth no less
> Than all that way and weariness ?"

There is a noble subtlety in this last stanza which is far above conceits. Otherwise the precise turn of thought would never have reappeared after nearly two and a half centuries in Cust's ardently sincere poem *Non Nobis*.

> " May light and life and earth and sky be blasted,
>   But let not all that wealth of love be wasted :
>   Let Hell afford
>   The pavement of her Heaven ! "

Crashaw's poems were published in 1646, four years before Vaughan's. In the interim appeared the *Noble Numbers* of Robert Herrick, a volume of consummate verse differing in one most curious respect from all the religious poetry of that generation ; for it was the work of one who was at least as much devoted to the Pagan as to the Christian ideal of life. In the *Noble Numbers* we do not, it is true, see Herrick as the old Roman Epicurean idling delicately with his bevy of imaginary mistresses, and refusing for himself all the sensuous delights of earth. But the same qualities go to the making of the man in his devotions and in his more frequent Hesperidean moments. It has been wittily said that his marvellous charm is made up of the union of a classical ear and a modern eye : his style is an antique setting for the old English life which he knew in its homeliest country quarters. In the remote vicarage of Dean Prior, where he lived from 1629 to 1648, and again from 1662 to his death in 1674, he was at times intolerant of his rustic neighbours and their stagnant backwater of life ; but he mingled true touches of Devon with his fine Horatian measures. So doing he came near to George Herbert : the sudden strokes of realism breaking serious thought or stately expression into what is called " quaintness." A characteristic example is his *Thanksgiving to God, for his House*, wherein he gives thanks not only for house, chamber, safe sleep, harmless thoughts, and ministra- tion to the poor, but also for his dinner—

> " The worts, the purslain, and the messe
>   Of water-cresse
>   Which of Thy kindnesse Thou hast sent ;
>   And my content
>   Makes those, and my beloved beet,
>   To be more sweet "

Charming as this simplicity is, it has hardly the con-
vincing power of Herbert's : there is just too much art
in it. But for music, and all that music gives, Herrick
is unsurpassed. In the poem beginning " Night hath
no wings to him that cannot sleep," even quaintness is
used as no one else could use it.

> " Sick is my heart ! O Saviour, do Thou please
>   To make my bed soft in my sicknesses :
>   Lighten my candle, so that I beneath
>   Sleep not for ever in the vaults of death."

Equal to this is Herrick's *Litany to the Holy Spirit,* and
beyond it, *The White Island : or Place of the Blest,* whose
very first stanza shows us a Herrick elsewhere unknown :

> " In this world, the isle of dreams,
>   While we sit by sorrow's streams,
>   Tears and terrors are our themes
>   Reciting ; "

for we find him here far nearer to " Young Eternity,"

> " In that whiter island, where
>   Things are evermore sincere."

Henry Vaughan's *Silex Scintillans* appeared in 1650–1,
two years after Herrick's poems. He too was a Royalist,
and is thought to have served for a time in the King's
army, after leaving Jesus College, Oxford. During two
years of the Protectorate he retired to Brecon and
practised medicine. It has long been the custom to
compare him with Herbert, and to find him inferior ;

but this is an incomplete statement of his position. He was, obviously and avowedly, a follower along a path already discovered and well trodden; but no follower has ever made better use of his advantage. Herbert keeps a fairer level, both in wit and in simplicity; but Vaughan's successes are far beyond that level. *The Retreat, Peace, The Dawning, Man, They are all gone into the World of Light, Quickness, The Waterfall,*—these are poems which can never be displaced, nor outmatched even by Herbert's *Easter, Sinne, Prayer, Love, Con-stancie, The Pulley,* and *The Elixer*. The truth is that they are not imitations, any more than the gifts of a son are imitations of the father who begat him. And in this case if the father was the wittier and the more original, the son is beyond dispute the deeper mind.

Vaughan's mantle fell in turn upon another young Oxonian, Thomas Traherne of Brasenose College, after-wards Rector of Credenhill near Hereford, and finally Vicar of Teddington till his death in 1674. The greater part of his poems remained unpublished until some of them were discovered in 1903 by Mr. Bertram Dobell, and others in 1910 by Mr. H. T. Ball. They show a very close study of both Herbert and Vaughan, and a devo-tion to the latter which is interesting because it reveals an intellectual rather than a verbal or metrical disciple-ship. Traherne's metres are ineffective, and perhaps the worst is that used in *The Apostacy,* where Herbert's defects are carefully copied. But from Vaughan he learnt to brood on childhood and the child's vision of the world, into which he has descended from Eternity.

> "How like an angel came I down !
>   How bright are all things here !
> When first among his works I did appear
>   O how their glory did me crown !
> The World resembled his Eternity
>   In which my soul did walk ;
>   And everything that I did see
>   Did with me talk."

This poem (*Wonder*) and the similar one called *Christendom* are Traherne's best ; though in others he has some real felicities here and there, as in *Dumness*, where he speaks of Eternal Bliss :

> " D'ye ask me what ? It was for to admire
> The Satisfaction of all Just Desire ; "

and in *Nature*, where he calls Infinity

> " A secret Self I had enclos'd within
> That was not bounded by my cloaths or skin
> Or terminated with my Sight, whose Sphere
> Ran parallel with that of Heaven here."

But we feel as we read his pages that the tide is ebbing : Traherne's is a real wave but a small one, and it does not come near the shore-line of its forerunners. And the ebb is in no way to be regretted, for other tides will break upon other sands of Time. The value of the 16th-century devotional poets is not diminished by the certainty which we feel that we shall never again see their like. Herbert, Crashaw, Vaughan, and Traherne are none of them men of our time : we love their sincerity and the beauty of their voices, but we receive a part only of their devotional spirit, because they are speaking of religion, and religion is everywhere and under all forms a unique and individual relation—the ways to God are as many as the souls of men. The personal truth of these poets is that which remains with us : the point of view of a past age can hardly be our own, but sincerity will always be the first necessity of poetry. Herrick too belongs to the past ; but his verse is imperishable. Time may destroy the content of a poem, but a perfect form is inexhaustible. What Herrick took from Ben Jonson and from Horace may yet be the freedom of many poets in many years. Of Donne we must give a different account : his form of expression has stood between him and many readers. But he is nevertheless a modern poet, a man of our own time and of times to come, and at his greatest he has a power of expression which can only be described by saying that it is the thoughts of the imagination of his heart made audible. To judge of the ardour, the weight, the swift subtlety of those thoughts we have only to read the *Holy Sonnets*, and in particular the Vth, VIth, and VIIth of them; the Litany, and especially the XVth, XVIth, XXth, and XXIIIrd petitions of it; and the three stanzas of the *Hymn to God the Father*. When there shall come another religious poet as great as Donne, he will speak like him : not because the content or the form of his verse will be like his, but because those to whom he speaks will forget the content and the form in the reality of the experience.

HENRY NEWBOLT

JOHN DONNE

DIVINE POEMS

TO THE E[ARL] OF D[ONCASTER]:
WITH SIX HOLY SONNETS

SEE, sir, how, as the sun's hot masculine flame
   Begets strange creatures on Nile's dirty slime,
   In me your fatherly yet lusty rhyme
—For these songs are their fruits—have wrought the
      same.
But though th' engend'ring force from which they came
   Be strong enough, and Nature doth admit
   Seven to be born at once ; I send as yet
But six ; they say the seventh hath still some maim.
   I choose your judgment, which the same degree
Doth with her sister, your invention, hold,
   As fire these drossy rhymes to purify,
Or as elixir, to change them to gold.
   You are that alchemist, which always had
   Wit, whose one spark could make good things of bad.

LA CORONA

1. *Deign at my hands this crown of prayer and praise,*
   Weaved in my lone devout melancholy,

Thou which of good hast, yea, art treasury,
All changing unchanged Ancient of days.
But do not with a vile crown of frail bays
Reward my Muse's white sincerity ;
But what Thy thorny crown gain'd, that give me,
A crown of glory, which doth flower always.
The ends crown our works, but Thou crown'st our
    ends,
For at our ends begins our endless rest.
The first last end, now zealously possess'd,
With a strong sober thirst my soul attends.
'Tis time that heart and voice be lifted high ;
Salvation to all that will is nigh.

ANNUNCIATION

2. *Salvation to all that will is nigh ;*
That All, which always is all everywhere,
Which cannot sin, and yet all sins must bear,
Which cannot die, yet cannot choose but die,
Lo ! faithful Virgin, yields Himself to lie
In prison, in thy womb ; and though He there
Can take no sin, nor thou give, yet He'll wear,
Taken from thence, flesh, which death's force may try.
Ere by the spheres time was created thou
Wast in His mind, who is thy Son, and Brother ;
Whom thou conceivest, conceived ; yea, thou art now
Thy Maker's maker, and thy Father's mother.
Thou hast light in dark, and shutt'st in little room
Immensity, cloister'd in thy dear womb.

NATIVITY

3. *Immensity, cloister'd in thy dear womb,*
Now leaves His well-beloved imprisonment.
There he hath made himself to his intent

Weak enough, now into our world to come.
But O ! for thee, for Him, hath th' inn no room ?
Yet lay Him in this stall, and from th' orient,
Stars, and wise men will travel to prevent
The effects of Herod's jealous general doom.
See'st thou, my soul, with thy faith's eye, how He
Which fills all place, yet none holds Him, doth lie ?
Was not His pity towards thee wondrous high,
That would have need to be pitied by thee ?
Kiss Him, and with Him into Egypt go,
With His kind mother, who partakes thy woe.

TEMPLE

4. *With His kind mother, who partakes thy woe,*
Joseph, turn back ; see where your child doth sit,
Blowing, yea blowing out those sparks of wit,
Which Himself on the doctors did bestow.
The Word but lately could not speak, and lo !
It suddenly speaks wonders ; whence comes it,
That all which was, and all which should be writ,
A shallow seeming child should deeply know ?
His Godhead was not soul to His manhood,
Nor had time mellow'd Him to this ripeness ;
But as for one which hath a long task, 'tis good,
With the sun to begin His business,
He in His age's morning thus began,
By miracles exceeding power of man.

CRUCIFYING

5. *By miracles exceeding power of man,*
He faith in some, envy in some begat,
For, what weak spirits admire, ambitious hate ,
In both affections many to Him ran.
But O ! the worst are most, they will and can

Alas ! and do, unto th' Immaculate,
Whose creature Fate is, now prescribe a fate,
Measuring self-life's infinity to span,
Nay to an inch.   Lo ! where condemned He
Bears His own cross, with pain, yet by and by
When it bears him, He must bear more and die.
Now Thou art lifted up, draw me to Thee,
And at Thy death giving such liberal dole,
Moist with one drop of Thy blood my dry soul.

RESURRECTION

6. *Moist with one drop of Thy blood, my dry soul*
Shall—though she now be in extreme degree
Too stony hard, and yet too fleshly—be
Freed by that drop, from being starved, hard or foul,
And life by this death abled shall control
Death, whom Thy death slew ; nor shall to me
Fear of first or last death bring misery,
If in Thy life-book my name thou enroll.
Flesh in that long sleep is not putrified,
But made that there, of which, and for which it was ;
Nor can by other means be glorified.
May then sin's sleep and death soon from me pass,
That waked from both, I again risen may
Salute the last and everlasting day.

ASCENSION

7. *Salute the last and everlasting day,*
Joy at th' uprising of this Sun, and Son,
Ye whose true tears, or tribulation
Have purely wash'd, or burnt your drossy clay.
Behold, the Highest, parting hence away,
Lightens the dark clouds, which He treads upon ;
Nor doth He by ascending show alone,

But first He and He first enters the way.
O strong Ram, which hast batter'd heaven for me !
Mild Lamb, which with Thy Blood hast mark'd the
     path !
Bright Torch, which shinest, that I the way may see !
O, with Thy own Blood quench Thy own just wrath ;
And if Thy Holy Spirit my Muse did raise,
Deign at my hands this crown of prayer and praise.

TO THE LADY MAGDALEN HERBERT, OF
ST. MARY MAGDALEN

HER of your name, whose fair inheritance
    Bethina was, and jointure Magdalo,
An active faith so highly did advance,
    That she once knew, more than the Church did know,
The Resurrection ; so much good there is
    Deliver'd of her, that some Fathers be
Loth to believe one woman could do this ;
    But think these Magdalens were two or three.
Increase their number, Lady, and their fame ;
    To their devotion add your innocence ;
Take so much of th' example as of the name,
    The latter half ; and in some recompense,
That they did harbour Christ Himself, a guest,
    Harbour these hymns, to His dear Name address'd.

HOLY SONNETS

I

THOU hast made me, and shall Thy work decay ?
Repair me now, for now mine end doth haste ;
I run to death, and Death meets me as fast,
And all my pleasures are like yesterday.
I dare not move my dim eyes any way ;

Despair behind, and Death before doth cast
Such terror, and my feeble flesh doth waste
By sin in it, which it towards hell doth weigh.
Only Thou art above, and when towards Thee
By Thy leave I can look, I rise again ;
But our old subtle foe so tempteth me,
That not one hour myself I can sustain.
Thy grace may wing me to prevent his art
And thou like adamant draw mine iron heart.

II

As due by many titles I resign
Myself to thee, O God.   First I was made
By Thee ; and for Thee, and when I was decay'd
Thy blood bought that, the which before was Thine.
I am Thy son, made with Thyself to shine,
Thy servant, whose pains Thou hast still repaid,
Thy sheep, Thine image, and—till I betray'd
Myself—a temple of Thy Spirit divine.
Why doth the devil then usurp on me ?
Why doth he steal, nay ravish, that's Thy right ?
Except Thou rise and for Thine own work fight,
O ! I shall soon despair, when I shall see
That Thou lovest mankind well, yet wilt not choose me,
And Satan hates me, yet is loth to lose me.

III

O ! might those sighs and tears return again
Into my breast and eyes, which I have spent,
That I might in this holy discontent
Mourn with some fruit, as I have mourn'd in vain.
In mine idolatry what showers of rain
Mine eyes did waste ? what griefs my heart did rent ?
That sufferance was my sin, I now repent ;
'Cause I did suffer, I must suffer pain.
Th' hydroptic drunkard, and night-scouting thief,

The itchy lecher, and self-ticking proud
Have the remembrance of past joys, for relief
Of coming ills.   To poor me is allow'd
No ease ; for long, yet vehement grief hath been
Th' effect and cause, the punishment and sin.

IV

O, my black soul, now thou art summoned
By sickness, Death's herald and champion ;
Thou'rt like a pilgrim, which abroad hath done
Treason, and durst not turn to whence he's fled ;
Or like a thief, which till death's doom be read,
Wisheth himself deliver'd from prison,
But damn'd and haled to execution,
Wisheth that still he might be imprisoned.
Yet grace, if thou repent, thou canst not lack ;
But who shall give thee that grace to begin ?
O, make thyself with holy mourning black,
And red with blushing, as thou art with sin ;
Or wash thee in Christ's blood, which hath this might,
That being red, it dyes red souls to white.

V

I am a little world made cunningly
Of elements, and an angelic sprite ;
But black sin hath betray'd to endless night
My world's both parts, and, O, both parts must die.
You which beyond that heaven which was most high
Have found new spheres, and of new land can write
Pour new seas in my eyes, that so I might
Drown my world with my weeping earnestly,
Or wash it if it must be drown'd no more.
But, O, it must be burnt ; alas ! the fire
Of lust and envy burnt it heretofore,
And made it fouler ; let their flames retire,
(2,654)

And burn me, O Lord, with a fiery zeal
Of Thee and Thy house, which doth in eating heal.

VI

This is my play's last scene ; here heavens appoint
My pilgrimage's last mile ; and my race
Idly, yet quickly run, hath this last pace ;
My span's last inch, my minutes' latest point ;
And gluttonous Death will instantly unjoint
My body and soul, and I shall sleep a space ;
But my ever-waking part shall see that face,
Whose fear already shakes my every joint.
Then, as my soul to heaven her first seat takes flight,
And earth-born body in the earth shall dwell,
So fall my sins, that all may have their right,
To where they're bred and would press me to hell.
Impute me righteous, thus purged of evil,
For thus I leave the world, the flesh, the devil.

VII

At the round earth's imagined corners blow
Your trumpets, angels, and arise, arise
From death, you numberless infinities
Of souls, and to your scattered bodies go ;
All whom the flood did, and fire shall o'erthrow,
All whom war, death, age, agues, tyrannies,
Despair, law, chance hath slain, and you, whose eyes
Shall behold God, and never taste death's woe.
But let them sleep, Lord, and me mourn a space ;
For, if above all these my sins abound,
'Tis late to ask abundance of Thy grace,
When we are there.   Here on this lowly ground,
Teach me how to repent, for that's as good
As if Thou hadst seal'd my pardon with Thy blood.

VIII

If faithful souls be alike glorified
As angels, then my father's soul doth see,
And adds this even to full felicity,
That valiantly I hell's wide mouth o'erstride.
But if our minds to these souls be descried
By circumstances, and by signs that be
Apparent in us not immediately,
How shall my mind's white truth by them be tried?
They see idolatrous lovers weep and mourn,
And stile blasphemous conjurers to call
On Jesu's name, and pharisaical
Dissemblers feign devotion. Then turn,
O pensive soul, to God, for He knows best
Thy grief, for He put it into my breast.

IX

If poisonous minerals, and if that tree,
Whose fruit threw death on (else immortal) us,
If lecherous goats, if serpents envious
Cannot be damn'd, alas! why should I be?
Why should intent or reason, born in me,
Make sins, else equal, in me more heinous?
And, mercy being easy, and glorious
To God, in His stern wrath why threatens He?
But who am I, that dare dispute with Thee?
O God, O! of Thine only worthy blood,
And my tears, make a heavenly Lethean flood,
And drown in it my sin's black memory.
That Thou remember them, some claim as debt;
I think it mercy if Thou wilt forget.

X

Death, be not proud, though some have called thee
Mighty and dreadful, for thou art not so;

For those, whom thou think'st thou dost overthrow,
Die not, poor Death, nor yet canst thou kill me.
From rest and sleep, which but thy picture be,
Much pleasure, then from thee much more must flow,
And soonest our best men with thee do go,
Rest of their bones, and soul's delivery.
Thou'rt slave to Fate, chance, kings, and desperate men,
And dost with poison, war, and sickness dwell,
And poppy, or charms can make us sleep as well,
And better than thy stroke ; why swell'st thou then ?
One short sleep past, we wake eternally,
And Death shall be no more ; Death, thou shalt die.

XI

Spit in my face, you Jews, and pierce my side,
Buffet, and scoff, scourge, and crucify me,
For I have sinn'd, and sinn'd, and only He,
Who could do no iniquity, hath died.
But by my death can not be satisfied
My sins, which pass the Jews' impiety.
They kill'd once an inglorious man, but I
Crucify him daily, being now glorified.
O let me then His strange love still admire ;
Kings pardon, but He bore our punishment ;
And Jacob came clothed in vile harsh attire,
But to supplant, and with gainful intent ;
God clothed Himself in vile man's flesh, that so
He might be weak enough to suffer woe.

XII

Why are we by all creatures waited on ?
Why do the prodigal elements supply
Life and food to me, being more pure than I,
Simpler and further from corruption ?
Why brook'st thou, ignorant horse, subjection ?
Why dost thou, bull and boar, so sillily
Dissemble weakness, and by one man's stroke die,

Whose whole kind you might swallow and feed upon ?
Weaker I am, woe's me, and worse than you ;
You have not sinn'd, nor need be timorous.
But wonder at a greater, for to us
Created nature doth these things subdue ;
But their Creator, whom sin, nor nature tied,
For us, His creatures, and His foes, hath died.

XIII

What if this present were the world's last night ?
Mark in my heart, O soul, where thou dost dwell,
The picture of Christ crucified, and tell
Whether His countenance can thee affright.
Tears in His eyes quench the amazing light ;
Blood fills his frowns, which from His pierced head fell ;
And can that tongue adjudge thee unto hell,
Which pray'd forgiveness for His foes' fierce spite ?
No, no ; but as in my idolatry
I said to all my profane mistresses,
Beauty of pity, foulness only is
A sign of rigour ; so I say to thee,
To wicked spirits are horrid shapes assign'd ;
This beauteous form assumes a piteous mind.

XIV

Batter my heart, three-person'd God ; for you
As yet but knock ; breathe, shine, and seek to mend ;
That I may rise, and stand, o'erthrow me, and bend
Your force, to break, blow, burn, and make me new.
I, like an usurp'd town, to another due,
Labour to admit you, but O, to no end,
Reason, your viceroy in me, me should defend,
But is captived, and proves weak or untrue.
Yet dearly I love you, and would be loved fain,
But am betroth'd unto your enemy ;
Divorce me, untie, or break that knot again,

Take me to you, imprison me, for I,
Except you enthrall me, never shall be free,
Nor ever chaste, except you ravish me.

XV

Wilt thou love God as He thee ? then digest,
My soul, this wholesome meditation,
How God the Spirit, by angels waited on
In heaven, doth make His temple in thy breast.
The Father having begot a Son most blest,
And still begetting—for he ne'er begun—
Hath deign'd to choose thee by adoption,
Co-heir to His glory, and Sabbath's endless rest.
And as a robb'd man, which by search doth find
His stolen stuff sold, must lose or buy it again,
The Sun of glory came down, and was slain,
Us whom He had made, and Satan stole, to unbind.
'Twas much, that man was made like God before,
But, that God should be made like man, much more.

XVI

Father, part of His double interest
Unto Thy kingdom Thy Son gives to me ;
His jointure in the knotty Trinity
He keeps, and gives to me his death's conquest.
This Lamb, whose death with life the world hath blest,
Was from the world's beginning slain, and He
Hath made two wills, which with the legacy
Of His and Thy kingdom do thy sons invest.
Yet such are these laws, that men argue yet
Whether a man those statutes can fulfil.
None doth ; but thy all-healing grace and Spirit
Revive again what law and letter kill.
Thy laws abridgement, and Thy last command
Is all but love ; O let this last Will stand !

THE CROSS

Since Christ embraced the cross itself, dare I
His image, th' image of His cross, deny?
Would I have profit by the sacrifice,
And dare the chosen altar to despise?
It bore all other sins, but is it fit
That it should bear the sin of scorning it?
Who from the picture would avert his eye,
How would he fly his pains who there did die?
From me no pulpit, nor misgrounded law,
Nor scandal taken, shall this cross withdraw,
It shall not, for it cannot; for the loss
Of this cross were to me another cross.
Better were worse, for no affliction,
No cross is so extreme, as to have none.
Who can blot out the cross, which th' instrument
Of God dew'd on me in the Sacrament?
Who can deny me power, and liberty
To stretch mine arms, and mine own cross to be?
Swim, and at every stroke thou art thy cross;
The mast and yard make one, where seas do toss;
Look down, thou spiest out crosses in small things;
Look up, thou seest birds raised on crossed wings;
All the globe's frame, and spheres, is nothing else
But the meridians crossing parallels.
Material crosses then good physic be,
But yet spiritual have chief dignity.
These for extracted chemic medicine serve,
And cure much better, and as well preserve.
Then are you your own physic, or need none,
When still'd or purged by tribulation;
For when that cross ungrudged unto you sticks,
Then are you to yourself a crucifix.
As perchance carvers do not faces make,
But that away, which hid them there, do take;

Let crosses, so, take what hid Christ in thee,
And be His image, or not His, but He.
But, as oft alchemists do coiners prove,
So may a self-despising get self-love ;
And then, as worst surfeits of best meats be,
So is pride, issued from humility,
For 'tis no child, but monster ; therefore cross
Your joy in crosses, else 'tis double loss.
And cross thy senses, else both they and thou
Must perish soon, and to destruction bow.
For if the eye seek good objects, and will take
No cross from bad, we cannot 'scape a snake.
So with harsh, hard, sour, stinking ; cross the rest ;
Make them indifferent ; call, nothing best.
But most the eye needs crossing, that can roam,
And move ; to th' others th' objects must come home.
And cross thy heart ; for that in man alone
Pants downwards, and hath palpitation.
Cross those dejections, when it downward tends,
And when it to forbidden heights pretends.
And as the brain through bony walls doth vent
By sutures, which a cross's form present,
So when thy brain works, ere thou utter it,
Cross and correct concupiscence of wit.
Be covetous of crosses ; let none fall ;
Cross no man else, but cross thyself in all.
Then doth the cross of Christ work faithfully
Within our hearts, when we love harmlessly
The cross's pictures much, and with more care
That cross's children, which our crosses are.

RESURRECTION, IMPERFECT

SLEEP, sleep, old sun, thou canst not have repass'd,
As yet, the wound thou took'st on Friday last ;
Sleep then, and rest ; the world may bear thy stay ;
A better sun rose before thee to-day ;

Who—not content to enlighten all that dwell
On the earth's face, as thou—enlighten'd hell,
And made the dark fires languish in that vale,
As at thy presence here our fires grow pale ;
Whose body, having walk'd on earth, and now
Hasting to heaven, would—that He might allow
Himself unto all stations, and fill all—
For these three days become a mineral.
He was all gold when He lay down, but rose
All tincture, and doth not alone dispose
Leaden and iron wills to good, but is
Of power to make e'en sinful flesh like his.
Had one of those, whose credulous piety
Thought that a soul one might discern and see
Go from a body, at this sepulchre been,
And, issuing from the sheet, this body seen,
He would have justly thought this body a soul,
If not of any man, yet of the whole.

Desunt Caetera.

THE ANNUNCIATION AND PASSION

TAMELY, frail body, abstain to-day ; to-day
My soul eats twice, Christ hither and away.
She sees Him man, so like God made in this,
That of them both a circle emblem is,
Whose first and last concur ; this doubtful day
Of feast or fast, Christ came, and went away ;
She sees Him nothing, twice at once, who's all ;
She sees a cedar plant itself, and fall ;
Her Maker put to making, and the head
Of life at once not yet alive, yet dead ;
She sees at once the Virgin Mother stay
Recluded at home, public at Golgotha ;
Sad and rejoiced she's seen at once, and seen
At almost fifty, and at scarce fifteen ;

At once a son is promised her, and gone ;
Gabriel gives Christ to her, He her to John ;
Not fully a mother, she's in orbity ;
At once receiver and the legacy.
All this, and all between, this day hath shown,
Th' abridgement of Christ's story, which makes one—
As in plain maps, the furthest west is east—
Of th' angels *Ave*, and *Consummatum est.*
How well the Church, God's Court of Faculties,
Deals, in sometimes, and seldom joining these.
As by the self-fix'd Pole we never do
Direct our course, but the next star thereto,
Which shows where th' other is, and which we say
—Because it strays not far—doth never stray,
So God by His Church, nearest to him, we know,
And stand firm, if we by her motion go.
His Spirit, as His fiery pillar, doth
Lead, and His Church, as cloud ; to one end both.
This Church by letting those days join, hath shown
Death and conception in mankind is one ;
Or 'twas in Him the same humility,
That He would be a man, and leave to be ;
Or as creation He hath made, as God,
With the last judgment but one period,
His imitating spouse would join in one
Manhood's extremes ; He shall come, He is gone ;
Or as though one blood drop, which thence did fall,
Accepted, would have served, He yet shed all,
So though the least of His pains, deeds, or words,
Would busy a life, she all this day affords.
This treasure then, in gross, my soul, uplay,
And in my life retail it every day.

GOOD-FRIDAY, 1613, RIDING WESTWARD

Let man's soul be a sphere, and then, in this,
Th' intelligence that moves, devotion is ;

And as the other spheres, by being grown
Subject to foreign motion, lose their own,
And being by others hurried every day,
Scarce in a year their natural form obey ;
Pleasure or business, so, our souls admit
For their first mover, and are whirl'd by it.
Hence is't, that I am carried towards the west,
This day, when my soul's form bends to the East.
There I should see a Sun by rising set,
And by that setting endless day beget.
But that Christ on His cross did rise and fall,
Sin had eternally benighted all.
Yet dare I almost be glad, I do not see
That spectacle of too much weight for me.
Who sees God's face, that is self-life, must die ;
What a death were it then to see God die ?
It made His own lieutenant, Nature, shrink,
It made His footstool crack, and the sun wink.
Could I behold those hands, which span the poles
And tune all spheres at once, pierced with those holes ?
Could I behold that endless height, which is
Zenith to us and our antipodes,
Humbled below us ? or that blood, which is
The seat of all our souls, if not of His,
Made dirt of dust, or that flesh which was worn
By God for His apparel, ragg'd and torn ?
If on these things I durst not look, durst I
On His distressed Mother cast mine eye,
Who was God's partner here, and furnish'd thus
Half of that sacrifice which ransom'd us ?
Though these things as I ride be from mine eye,
They're present yet unto my memory,
For that looks towards them ; and Thou look'st towards
     me,
O Saviour, as Thou hang'st upon the tree.
I turn my back to Thee but to receive
Corrections till Thy mercies bid Thee leave.
O think me worth Thine anger, punish me,

Burn off my rust, and my deformity ;
Restore Thine image, so much, by Thy grace,
That Thou mayst know me, and I'll turn my face.

A LITANY

I

THE FATHER

FATHER of Heaven, and Him, by whom
It, and us for it, and all else for us,
    Thou madest and govern'st ever, come
And re-create me, now grown ruinous.
        My heart is by dejection, clay,
            And by self-murder, red.
From this red earth, O Father, purge away
All vicious tinctures, that new-fashioned
I may rise up from death, before I'm dead.

II

THE SON

O Son of God, who, seeing two things,
Sin and Death, crept in, which were never made,
    By bearing one, tried'st with what stings
The other could Thine heritage invade ;
        O be Thou nail'd unto my heart,
            And crucified again ;
Part not from it, though it from Thee would part,
But let it be by applying so Thy pain,
Drown'd in Thy blood, and in Thy passion slain.

III

THE HOLY GHOST

O Holy Ghost, whose temple I
Am, but of mud walls, and condensèd dust,

And being sacrilegiously
Half wasted with youth's fires of pride and lust,
    Must with new storms be weather-beat,
    Double in my heart Thy flame,
Which let devout sad tears intend, and let—
Though this glass lanthorn, flesh, do suffer maim—
Fire, sacrifice, priest, altar be the same.

IV

THE TRINITY

O blessed glorious Trinity,
Bones to philosophy, but milk to faith,
    Which, as wise serpents, diversely
Most slipperiness, yet most entanglings hath,
    As you distinguish'd, undistinct,
    By power, love, knowledge be,
Give me a such self different instinct,
Of these let all me elemented be,
Of power, to love, to know you unnumbered three.

V

THE VIRGIN MARY

For that fair blessed mother-maid,
Whose flesh redeem'd us, that she-cherubin,
    Which unlock'd paradise, and made
One claim for innocence, and disseizèd sin,
    Whose womb was a strange heaven, for there
    God clothed Himself, and grew,
Our zealous thanks we pour. As her deeds were
Our helps, so are her prayers ; nor can she sue
In vain, who hath such titles unto you.

VI

THE ANGELS

And since this life our nonage is,
And we in wardship to Thine angels be,
   Native in heaven's fair palaces
Where we shall be but denizen'd by Thee ;
       As this earth conceiving by the sun,
       Yields fair diversity,
Yet never knows what course that light doth run ;
So let me study that mine actions be
Worthy their sight, though blind in how they see.

VII

THE PATRIARCHS

And let Thy patriarchs' desire,
—Those great grandfathers of Thy Church, which saw
   More in the cloud than we in fire,
Whom nature clear'd more, than us grace and law,
       And now in heaven still pray, that we
       May use our new helps right—
Be satisfied, and fructify in me ;
Let not my mind be blinder by more light,
Nor faith by reason added lose her sight.

VIII

THE PROPHETS

Thy eagle-sighted prophets too,
—Which were Thy Church's organs, and did sound
   That harmony which made of two
One law, and did unite, but not confound ;

Those heavenly poets which did see
Thy will, and it express
In rhythmic feet—in common pray for me,
That I by them excuse not my excess
In seeking secrets, or poeticness.

IX

THE APOSTLES

And thy illustrious zodiac
Of twelve apostles, which engirt this All,
—From whom whosoever do not take
Their light, to dark deep pits throw down and fall ;—
      As through their prayers Thou'st let me know
      That their books are divine,
May they pray still, and be heard, that I go
Th' old broad way in applying ; O decline
Me, when my comment would make Thy word mine

X

THE MARTYRS

And since Thou so desirously
Didst long to die, that long before Thou couldst
And long since Thou no more couldst die,
Thou in thy scatter'd mystic body wouldst
      In Abel die, and ever since
      In Thine ; let their blood come
To beg for us a discreet patience
Of death, or of worse life ; for O, to some
Not to be martyrs, is a martyrdom.

XI

THE CONFESSORS

Therefore with Thee triumpheth there
A virgin squadron of white confessors,

Whose bloods betroth'd not married were,
Tender'd, not taken by those ravishers.
          They know, and pray that we may know,
            In every Christian
Hourly tempestuous persecutions grow ;
Temptations martyr us alive ; a man
Is to himself a Diocletian.

XII

THE VIRGINS

  The cold white snowy nunnery,
Which, as Thy Mother, their high abbess, sent
    Their bodies back again to Thee,
As Thou hadst lent them, clean and innocent ;
         Though they have not obtain'd of Thee,
         That or Thy Church or I
Should keep, as they, our first integrity,
Divorce Thou sin in us, or bid it die,
And call chaste widowhead virginity.

XIII

THE DOCTORS

  The sacred academy above
Of doctors, whose pains have unclasp'd, and taught
    Both books of life to us—for love
To know Thy scriptures tells us, we are wrote
         In Thy other book—pray for us there,
         That what they have misdone
Or missaid, we to that may not adhere.
Their zeal may be our sin.   Lord, let us run
Mean ways, and call them stars, but not the sun.

XIV

And whilst this universal quire,
That Church in triumph, this in warfare here,
    Warm'd with one all-partaking fire
Of love, that none be lost, which cost Thee dear,
            Prays ceaselessly, and Thou hearken too
                —Since to be gracious
Our task is treble, to pray, bear, and do—
Hear this prayer, Lord ; O Lord, deliver us
From trusting in those prayers, though pour'd out thus.

XV

From being anxious, or secure,
Dead clods of sadness, or light squibs of mirth,
    From thinking that great courts immure
All, or no happiness, or that this earth
            Is only for our prison framed,
                Or that Thou'rt covetous
To them whom Thou lovest, or that they are maim'd
From reaching this world's sweet who seek Thee thus,
With all their might, good Lord, deliver us.

XVI

From needing danger, to be good,
From owing Thee yesterday's tears to-day,
    From trusting so much to Thy blood
That in that hope we wound our soul away,
            From bribing Thee with alms, to excuse
                Some sin more burdenous,
From light affecting, in religion, news,
From thinking us all soul, neglecting thus
Our mutual duties, Lord, deliver us.

XVII

From tempting Satan to tempt us,
By our connivance, or slack company,
    From measuring ill by vicious
Neglecting to choke sin's spawn, vanity,
            From indiscreet humility,
            Which might be scandalous
And cast reproach on Christianity,
From being spies, or to spies pervious,
From thirst or scorn of fame, deliver us.

XVIII

Deliver us through Thy descent
Into the Virgin, whose womb was a place
    Of middle kind ; and Thou being sent
To ungracious us, stay'dst at her full of grace ;
            And through Thy poor birth, where first Thou
            Glorified'st poverty ;
And yet soon after riches didst allow,
By accepting kings' gifts in th' Epiphany ;
Deliver us, and make us to both ways free.

XIX

And through that bitter agony,
Which is still th' agony of pious wits,
    Disputing what distorted Thee,
And interrupted evenness with fits ;
            And through Thy free confession,
            Though thereby they were then
Made blind, so that Thou mightst from them have gone ;
Good Lord, deliver us, and teach us when
We may not, and we may, blind unjust men.

XX

Through Thy submitting all, to blows
Thy face, Thy robes to spoil, Thy fame to scorn,
   All ways, which rage, or justice knows,
And by which Thou couldst show that Thou wast born ;
        And through Thy gallant humbleness
        Which Thou in death didst show,
Dying before Thy soul they could express ;
Deliver us from death, by dying so
To this world, ere this world do bid us go.

XXI

When senses, which Thy soldiers are,
We arm against Thee, and they fight for sin ;
   When want, sent but to tame, doth war,
And work despair a breach to enter in ;
        When plenty, God's image, and seal,
        Makes us idolatrous,
And love it, not him, whom it should reveal ;
When we are moved to seem religious
Only to vent wit ; Lord, deliver us.

XXII

In churches, when th' infirmity
Of him which speaks, diminishes the word ;
   When magistrates do misapply
To us, as we judge, lay or ghostly sword ;
        When plague, which is Thine angel, reigns,
        Or wars, Thy champions, sway ;
When heresy, Thy second deluge, gains ;
In th' hour of death, th' eve of last Judgment day ;
Deliver us from the sinister way.

XXIII

Hear us, O hear us, Lord ; to Thee
A sinner is more music, when he prays,
   Than spheres' or angels' praises be,
In panegyric alleluias ;
        Hear us, for till Thou hear us, Lord,
        We know not what to say ;
Thine ear to our sighs, tears, thoughts, gives voice and
     word ;
O Thou, who Satan heard'st in Job's sick day,
Hear Thyself now, for Thou in us dost pray.

XXIV

That we may change to evenness
This intermitting aguish piety ;
   That snatching cramps of wickedness
And apoplexies of fast sin may die ;
        That music of Thy promises,
        Not threats in thunder may
Awaken us to our just offices ;
What in Thy book Thou dost, or creatures say,
That we may hear, Lord, hear us when we pray.

XXV

That our ears' sickness we may cure,
And rectify those labyrinths aright,
   That we by heark'ning not procure
Our praise, nor others' dispraise so invite ;
        That we get not a slipp'riness
        And senselessly decline,
From hearing bold wits jest at kings' excess,
To admit the like of majesty divine ;
That we may lock our ears, Lord, open Thine.

XXVI

That living law, the magistrate,
Which to give us, and make us physic, doth
   Our vices often aggravate ;
That preachers taxing sin, before her growth ;
       That Satan, and envenom'd men—
        Which will, if we starve, dine—
When they do most accuse us, may see then
Us to amendment hear them, Thee decline ;
That we may open our ears, Lord, lock Thine.

XXVII

That learning, Thine ambassador,
From Thine allegiance we never tempt ;
   That beauty, paradise's flower
For physic made, from poison be exempt ;
       That wit—born apt high good to do—
        By dwelling lazily
On nature's nothing be not nothing too ;
That our affections kill us not, nor die ;
Hear us, weak echoes, O, Thou Ear and Eye.

XXVIII

Son of God, hear us, and since Thou
By taking our blood, owest it us again,
   Gain to Thyself, and us allow ;
And let not both us and Thyself be slain ;
       O Lamb of God, which took'st our sin,
        Which could not stick to Thee,
O let it not return to us again ;
But patient and physician being free,
As sin is nothing, let it nowhere be.

UPON THE TRANSLATION OF THE PSALMS BY SIR PHILIP SIDNEY, AND THE COUNTESS OF PEMBROKE, HIS SISTER

ETERNAL God—for whom who ever dare
Seek new expressions, do the circle square,
And thrust into straight corners of poor wit
Thee, who art cornerless and infinite—
I would but bless Thy name, not name Thee now
—And Thy gifts are as infinite as Thou—
Fix we our praises therefore on this one,
That, as thy blessed Spirit fell upon
These Psalms' first author in a cloven tongue
—For 'twas a double power by which he sung
The highest matter in the noblest form—
So Thou hast cleft that Spirit, to perform
That work again, and shed it here, upon
Two, by their bloods, and by Thy Spirit one ;
A brother and a sister, made by Thee
The organ, where Thou art the harmony.
Two that make one John Baptist's holy voice,
And who that Psalm, " Now let the Isles rejoice,"
Have both translated, and applied it too,
Both told us what, and taught us how to do.
They show us islanders our Joy, our King ;
They tell us why, and teach us how to sing.
Make all this all three choirs, heaven, earth, and spheres ;
The first, Heaven, hath a song, but no man hears ;
The spheres have music, but they have no tongue,
Their harmony is rather danced than sung ;
But our third choir, to which the first gives ear
—For angels learn by what the Church does here—
This choir hath all.   The organist is he
Who hath tuned God and man, the organ we ;
The songs are these, which heaven's high holy Muse
Whisper'd to David, David to the Jews ;
And David's successors in holy zeal,

In forms of joy and art do re-reveal
To us so sweetly and sincerely too,
That I must not rejoice as I would do,
When I behold that these Psalms are become
So well attired abroad, so ill at home,
So well in chambers, in Thy Church so ill,
As I can scarce call that reform'd until
This be reform'd ; would a whole state present
A lesser gift than some one man hath sent ?
And shall our Church unto our Spouse and King
More hoarse, more harsh than any other, sing ?
For that we pray, we praise Thy name for this,
Which, by this Moses and this Miriam, is
Already done ; and as those Psalms we call,
—Though some have other authors—David's all,
So though some have, some may some Psalms translate,
We Thy Sidneian psalms shall celebrate,
And, till we come th' extemporal song to sing
—Learn'd the first hour that we see the King,
Who hath translated those translators—may
These their sweet learned labours all the way,
Be as our tuning, that when hence we part,
We may fall in with them, and sing our part !

ODE

1. VENGEANCE will sit above our faults ; but till
            She there do sit,
    We see her not, nor them.   Thus, blind, yet still
    We lead her way ; and thus, whilst we do ill,
            We suffer it.

2. Unhappy he whom youth makes not beware
            Of doing ill.
    Enough we labour under age, and care ;
    In number, th' errors of the last place are
            The greatest still.

3. Yet we, that should the ill we now begin
                As soon repent,
    Strange thing ! perceive not ; our faults are not seen,
    But past us ; neither felt, but only in
                The punishment.

4. But we know ourselves least ; mere outward shows
                Our minds so store,
    That our souls no more than our eyes disclose
    But form and colour.   Only he who knows
                Himself, knows more.

TO MR. TILMAN AFTER HE HAD TAKEN
ORDERS

Thou, whose diviner soul hath caused thee now
To put thy hand unto the holy plough,
Making lay-scornings of the ministry
Not an impediment, but victory ;
What bring'st thou home with thee ? how is thy mind
Affected since the vintage ?   Dost thou find
New thoughts and stirrings in thee ? and, as steel
Touch'd with a loadstone, dost new motions feel ?
Or, as a ship after much pain and care
For iron and cloth brings home rich Indian ware,
Hast thou thus traffick'd, but with far more gain
Of noble goods, and with less time and pain ?
Thou art the same materials, as before,
Only the stamp is changèd, but no more.
And as new crowned kings alter the face,
But not the money's substance, so hath grace
Changed only God's old image by creation,
To Christ's new stamp, at this thy coronation ;
Or, as we paint angels with wings, because
They bear God's message and proclaim His laws,

Since thou must do the like and so must move,
Art thou new feather'd with celestial love ?
Dear, tell me where thy purchase lies, and show
What thy advantage is above, below.
But if thy gainings do surmount expression,
Why doth the foolish world scorn that profession,
Whose joys pass speech ?   Why do they think unfit
That gentry should join families with it ?
As if their day were only to be spent
In dressing, mistressing and compliment.
Alas ! poor joys, but poorer men, whose trust
Seems richly placèd in sublimèd dust,
—For such are clothes and beauty, which though
    gay,
Are, at the best, but of sublimèd clay—
Let then the world thy calling disrespect,
But go thou on, and pity their neglect.
What function is so noble, as to be
Ambassador to God, and destiny ?
To open life ? to give kingdoms to more
Than kings give dignities ? to keep heaven's door ?
Mary's prerogative was to bear Christ, so
'Tis preachers' to convey Him, for they do,
As angels out of clouds, from pulpits speak ;
And bless the poor beneath, the lame, the weak.
If then th' astronomers, whereas they spy
A new-found star, their optics magnify,
How brave are those, who with their engine can
Bring man to heaven, and heaven again to man ?
These are thy titles and pre-eminences,
In whom must meet God's graces, men's offences ;
And so the heavens which beget all things here,
And th' earth, our mother, which these things doth
    bear ;
Both these in thee, are in thy calling knit
And make thee now a blest hermaphrodite.

A HYMN TO CHRIST, AT THE AUTHOR'S LAST GOING INTO GERMANY

In what torn ship so ever I embark,
That ship shall be my emblem of Thy ark;
What sea soever swallow me, that flood
Shall be to me an emblem of Thy blood;
Though Thou with clouds of anger do disguise
Thy face, yet through that mask I know those eyes,
   Which, though they turn away sometimes,
      They never will despise.

I sacrifice this island unto Thee,
And all whom I love there, and who love me;
When I have put our seas 'twixt them and me,
Put thou Thy seas betwixt my sins and Thee.
As the tree's sap doth seek the root below
In winter, in my winter now I go,
   Where none but Thee, the eternal root
      Of true love, I may know.

Nor Thou nor Thy religion dost control
The amorousness of an harmonious soul;
But Thou wouldst have that love Thyself; as Thou
Art jealous, Lord, so I am jealous now;
Thou lovest not, till from loving more Thou free
My soul; Who ever gives, takes liberty;
   Oh, if Thou carest not whom I love,
      Alas! Thou lovest not me.

Seal then this bill of my divorce to all,
On whom those fainter beams of love did fall;
Marry those loves, which in youth scatter'd be
On fame, wit, hopes—false mistresses—to Thee.
Churches are best for prayer, that have least light;
To see God only, I go out of sight;
   And to escape stormy days, I choose
      An everlasting night.

THE LAMENTATIONS OF JEREMY, FOR THE MOST PART ACCORDING TO TREMELLIUS

CHAP. I

1. How sits this city, late most populous,
   Thus solitary, and like a widow thus ?
   Amplest of nations, queen of provinces
   She was, who now thus tributary is ?

2. Still in the night she weeps, and her tears fall
   Down by her cheeks along, and none of all
   Her lovers comfort her ; perfidiously
   Her friends have dealt, and now are enemy.

3. Unto great bondage, and afflictions,
   Judah is captive led ; those nations
   With whom she dwells, no place of rest afford ;
   In straits she meets her persecutors' sword.

4. Empty are the gates of Sion, and her ways
   Mourn, because none come to her solemn days.
   Her priests do groan, her maids are comfortless ;
   And she's unto herself a bitterness.

5. Her foes are grown her head, and live at peace,
   Because, when her transgressions did increase,
   The Lord strook her with sadness ; the enemy
   Doth drive her children to captivity.

6. From Sion's daughter is all beauty gone ;
   Like harts which seek for pasture, and find none,
   Her princes are ; and now before the foe
   Which still pursues them, without strength they go.

7. Now in their days of tears, Jerusalem
   —Her men slain by the foe, none succouring them—

Remembers what of old she esteemed most,
Whiles her foes laugh at her, for what she hath lost.

8. Jerusalem hath sinn'd, therefore is she
Removed, as women in uncleanness be ;
Who honour'd, scorn her, for her foulness they
Have seen ; herself doth groan, and turn away.

9. Her foulness in her skirts was seen, yet she
Remember'd not her end ; miraculously
Therefore she fell, none comforting ; behold,
O Lord, my affliction, for the foe grows bold.

10. Upon all things where her delight hath been,
The foe hath stretch'd his hand, for she hath seen
Heathen, whom thou command'st should not do so,
Into her holy sanctuary go.

11. And all her people groan, and seek for bread ;
And they have given, only to be fed,
All precious things, wherein their pleasure lay ;
How cheap I'm grown, O Lord, behold, and weigh.

12. All this concerns not you, who pass by me ;
O see, and mark if any sorrow be
Like to my sorrow, which Jehovah hath
Done to me in the day of His fierce wrath ?

13. That fire, which by Himself is governed,
He hath cast from heaven on my bones, and spread
A net before my feet, and me o'erthrown,
And made me languish all the day alone.

14. His hand hath of my sins framèd a yoke
Which wreathed, and cast upon my neck, hath broke
My strength ; the Lord unto those enemies
Hath given me, from whom I cannot rise.

15. He under foot hath trodden in my sight
     My strong men ; He did company accite
     To break my young men ; He the winepress hath
     Trod upon Judah's daughter in His wrath.

16. For these things do I weep ; mine eye, mine eye
     Casts water out ; for He which should be nigh
     To comfort me, is now departed far ;
     The foe prevails, forlorn my children are.

17. There's none, though Sion do stretch out her hand,
     To comfort her ; it is the Lord's command
     That Jacob's foes girt him ; Jerusalem
     Is as an unclean woman amongst them.

18. But yet the Lord is just, and righteous still ;
     I have rebell'd against His holy will ;
     O hear all people, and my sorrow see,
     My maids, my young men in captivity.

19. I called for my lovers then, but they
     Deceived me, and my priests, and elders lay
     Dead in the city ; for they sought for meat
     Which should refresh their souls, and none could get.

20. Because I am in straits, Jehovah, see !
     My heart o'erturn'd, my bowels muddy be ;
     Because I have rebell'd so much, as fast
     The sword without, as death within, doth waste.

21. Of all which here I mourn, none comforts me ;
     My foes have heard my grief, and glad they be,
     That Thou hast done it ; but Thy promised day
     Will come, when, as I suffer, so shall they.

22. Let all their wickedness appear to Thee ;
     Do unto them, as Thou hast done to me,
     For all my sins ; the sighs which I have had
     Are very many, and my heart is sad.

CHAP. II

1. How over Sion's daughter hath God hung
   His wrath's thick cloud ? and from heaven hath flung
   To earth the beauty of Israel, and hath
   Forgot His foot-stool in the day of wrath ?

2. The Lord unsparingly hath swallowed
   All Jacob's dwellings, and demolished
   To ground the strength of Judah, and profaned
   The Princes of the kingdom, and the land.

3. In heat of wrath the horn of Israel He
   Hath clean cut off, and lest the enemy
   Be hinder'd, His right hand He doth retire,
   But is towards Jacob all-devouring fire.

4. Like to an enemy He bent His bow ;
   His right hand was in posture of a foe,
   To kill what Sion's daughter did desire,
   'Gainst whom His wrath He poured forth like fire.

5. For like an enemy Jehovah is,
   Devouring Israel, and his palaces,
   Destroying holds, giving additions
   To Judah's daughters' lamentations.

6. Like to a garden hedge He hath cast down
   The place where was His congregation,
   And Sion's feasts and sabbaths are forgot ;
   Her King, her Priest, His wrath regardeth not.

7. The Lord forsakes His altar, and detests
   His sanctuary, and in the foes' hands rests
   His palace, and the walls, in which their cries
   Are heard, as in the true solemnities.

8. The Lord hath cast a line, so to confound
   And level Sion's walls unto the ground;
   He draws not back His hand, which doth o'erturn
   The wall, and rampart, which together mourn.

9. Their gates are sunk into the ground, and He
   Hath broke the bar; their king and princes be
   Amongst the heathen, without law, nor there
   Unto their prophets doth the Lord appear.

10. There Sion's elders on the ground are placed,
    And silence keep; dust on their heads they cast;
    In sackcloth have they girt themselves, and low
    The virgins towards ground their heads do throw.

11. My bowels are grown muddy, and mine eyes
    Are faint with weeping; and my liver lies
    Pour'd out upon the ground, for misery
    That sucking children in the streets do die.

12. When they had cried unto their mothers, " Where
    Shall we have bread, and drink ? " they fainted there,
    And in the street like wounded persons lay,
    Till 'twixt their mothers' breasts they went away.

13. Daughter Jerusalem, O what may be
    A witness, or comparison for thee ?
    Sion, to ease thee, what shall I name like thee ?
    Thy breach is like the sea; what help can be ?

14. For thee vain foolish things thy prophets sought;
    Thee, thine iniquities they have not taught,
    Which might disturb thy bondage; but for thee
    False burthens, and false causes they would see.

15. The passengers do clap their hands, and hiss
    And wag their head at thee, and say, " Is this
    That city, which so many men did call
    Joy of the earth, and perfectest of all ? "

16. Thy foes do gape upon thee, and they hiss,
    And gnash their teeth, and say, " Devour we this,
    For this is certainly the day which we
    Expected, and which now we find, and see."

17. The Lord hath done that which He purposèd ;
    Fulfill'd His word of old determinèd ;
    He hath thrown down, and not spared, and thy foe
    Made glad above thee, and advanced him so.

18. But now their hearts unto the Lord do call ;
    Therefore, O walls of Sion, let tears fall
    Down like a river, day and night ; take thee
    No rest, but let thine eye incessant be.

19. Arise, cry in the night, pour out thy sins,
    Thy heart, like water, when the watch begins ;
    Lift up thy hands to God, lest children die,
    Which, faint for hunger, in the streets do lie.

20. Behold, O Lord, consider unto whom
    Thou hast done this ; what, shall the women come
    To eat their children of a span ? shall Thy
    Prophet and priest be slain in sanctuary ?

21. On ground in streets the young and old do lie
    My virgins and young men by sword do die ;
    Them in the day of Thy wrath Thou hast slain
    Nothing did Thee from killing them contain.

22. As to a solemn feast, all whom I fear'd
    Thou call'st about me ; when Thy wrath appear'd,
    None did remain or scape, for those which I
    Brought up, did perish by mine enemy.

CHAP. III

1. I am the man which have affliction seen,
   Under the rod of God's wrath having been ;
2. He hath led me to darkness, not to light,
3. And against me all day, His hand doth fight.

4. He hath broke my bones, worn out my flesh and skin,
5. Built up against me ; and hath girt me in
   With hemlock, and with labour ; 6. And set me
   In dark, as they who dead for ever be.

7. He hath hedged me lest I 'scape, and added more
   To my steel fetters heavier than before.
8. When I cry out He outshuts my prayer ; 9. And hath
   Stopp'd with hewn stone my way, and turn'd my path.

10. And like a lion hid in secrecy,
    Or bear which lies in wait, He was to me.
11. He stops my way, tears me, made desolate :
12. And He makes me the mark He shooteth at.

13. He made the children of His quiver pass
    Into my reins. 14. I, with my people, was
    All the day long, a song and mockery.
15. He hath fill'd me with bitterness, and He

    Hath made me drunk with wormwood. 16. He hath burst
    My teeth with stones, and cover'd me with dust.
17. And thus my soul far off from peace was set,
    And my prosperity I did forget.

18. My strength, my hope—unto myself I said—
    Which from the Lord should come, is perished :
19. But when my mournings I do think upon,
    My wormwood, hemlock, and affliction,

(2,654)

20. My soul is humbled in rememb'ring this ;
21. My heart considers, therefore, hope there is.
22. 'Tis God's great mercy we're not utterly
    Consumed, for His compassions do not die ;

23. For every morning they renewed be,
    For great, O Lord, is Thy fidelity.
24. The Lord is—saith my soul—my portion,
    And therefore in Him will I hope alone.

25. The Lord is good to them, who on Him rely,
    And to the soul that seeks Him earnestly.
26. It is both good to trust, and to attend
    The Lord's salvation unto the end.

27. 'Tis good for one His yoke in youth to bear.
28. He sits alone, and doth all speech forbear,
    Because he hath borne it.   29. And his mouth he lays
    Deep in the dust, yet then in hope he stays.

30. He gives his cheeks to whosoever will
    Strike him, and so he is reproached still.
31. For not for ever doth the Lord forsake ;
32. But when He hath struck with sadness, He doth take

    Compassion, as His mercy's infinite ;
33. Nor is it with His heart, that He doth smite,
34. That underfoot the prisoners stamped be,
35. That a man's right the judge himself doth see

    To be wrung from him ; 36. That he subverted is
    In his just cause, the Lord allows not this.
37. Who then will say, that aught doth come to pass,
    But that which by the Lord commanded was ?

38. Both good and evil from His mouth proceeds ;
39. Why then grieves any man for his misdeeds ?
40. Turn we to God, by trying out our ways ;
41. To Him in heav'n our hands with hearts upraise.

42. We have rebell'd, and fallen away from Thee ;
    Thou pardon'st not ; 43. Usest no clemency ;
    Pursuest us, kill'st us, cover'st us with wrath ;
44. Cover'st Thyself with clouds, that our prayer hath

    No power to pass. 45. And Thou hast made us fall
    As refuse, and off-scouring to them all.
46. All our foes gape at us. 47. Fear and a snare
    With ruin, and with waste upon us are.

48. With watery rivers doth mine eye o'erflow
    For ruin of my people's daughters so ;
49. Mine eye doth drop down tears incessantly,
50. Until the Lord look down from heav'n to see.

51. And for my city daughters' sake, mine eye
    Doth break mine heart. 52. Causeless mine enemy
    Like a bird chased me. 53. In a dungeon
    They've shut my life, and cast me on a stone.

54. Waters flow'd o'er my head ; then thought I, I am
    Destroy'd ; 55. I called, Lord, upon Thy name
    Out of the pit ; 56. And Thou my voice didst hear ;
    O from my sigh and cry, stop not Thine ear.

57. Then when I call'd upon Thee, Thou drew'st near
    Unto me, and said'st unto me, " Do not fear."
58. Thou, Lord, my soul's cause handled hast, and Thou
    Rescuest my life. 59. O Lord, do Thou judge now.

    Thou heardst my wrong, 60. Their vengeance, all
        they've wrought ;
61. How they reproach'd, Thou'st heard, and what they
        thought ;
62. What their lips utter'd, which against me rose,
    And what was ever whisper'd by my foes.

63. I am their song, whether they rise or sit ;
64. Give them rewards, Lord, for their working fit,
65. Sorrow of heart, Thy curse ; 66. And with Thy
      might
  Follow, and from under heaven destroy them quite.

CHAP. IV

1. How is the gold become so dim ?   How is
  Purest and finest gold thus changed to this ?
  The stones which were stones of the sanctuary,
  Scatter'd in corners of each street do lie.

2. The precious sons of Sion, which should be
  Valued at purest gold, how do we see
  Low rated now, as earthen pitchers, stand,
  Which are the work of a poor potter's hand ?

3. Even the sea-calfs draw their breasts, and give
  Suck to their young ; my people's daughters live,
  By reason of the foes' great cruelness,
  As do the owls in the vast wilderness.

4. And when the sucking child doth strive to draw,
  His tongue for thirst cleaves to his upper jaw ;
  And when for bread the children cry,
  There is no man that doth them satisfy.

5. They which before were delicately fed,
  Now in the streets forlorn have perished ;
  And they which ever were in scarlet clothed,
  Sit and embrace the dunghills which they loathed.

6. The daughters of my people have sinn'd more,
  Than did the town of Sodom sin before ;
  Which being at once destroy'd, there did remain
  No hands amongst them to vex them again.

7. But heretofore, purer her Nazarite
   Was than the snow, and milk was not so white ;
   As carbuncles did their pure bodies shine,
   And all their polish'dness was sapphirine.

8. They're darker now than blackness ; none can know
   Them by the face, as through the street they go ;
   For now their skin doth cleave unto their bone,
   And withered, is like to dry wood grown.

9. Better by sword than famine 'tis to die ;
   And better through-pierced, than through penury.
10. Women, by nature pitiful, have eat
    Their children—dress'd with their own hand—for meat.

11. Jehovah here fully accomplish'd hath
    His indignation, and pour'd forth His wrath ;
    Kindled a fire in Sion, which hath power
    To eat, and her foundations to devour.

12. Nor would the kings of th' earth, nor all which live
    In the inhabitable world believe,
    That any adversary, any foe,
    Into Jerusalem should enter so.

13. For the priests' sins, and prophets', which have shed
    Blood in the streets and the just murdered ;
14. Which, when those men whom they made blind did
    stray
    Thorough the streets, defilèd by the way

    With blood, the which impossible it was
    Their garment should 'scape touching as they pass
15. Would cry aloud, " Depart, defilèd men,
    Depart, depart, and touch not us ! " and then

    They fled, and stray'd, and with the Gentiles were ;
    Yet told their friends, they should not long dwell there.

16. For this they're scatter'd by Jehovah's face,
    Who never will regard them more ; no grace

    Unto their old men shall the foe afford ;
    Nor, that they're priests, redeem them from the sword.
17. And we as yet, for all these miseries
    Desiring our vain help, consume our eyes.

    And such a nation as cannot save,
    We in desire and speculation have ;
18. They hunt our steps, that in the streets we fear
    To go ; our end is now approached near.

    Our days accomplish'd are ; this the last day ;
    Eagles of heav'n are not so swift as they
19. Which follow us ; o'er mountain tops they fly
    At us, and for us in the desert lie.

20. Th' Anointed Lord, breath of our nostrils, He
    Of whom we said, under His shadow we
    Shall with more ease under the heathen dwell,
    Into the pit which these men digged, fell.

21. Rejoice, O Edom's daughter, joyful be
    Thou that inhabit'st Uz, for unto thee
    This cup shall pass, and thou with drunkenness
    Shalt fill thyself, and show thy nakedness.

22. Then thy sins, O Sion, shall be spent,
    The Lord will not leave thee in banishment.
    Thy sins, O Edom's daughter, He will see,
    And for them, pay thee with captivity.

CHAP. V

1. Remember, O Lord, what is fall'n on us ;
   See, and mark how we are reproached thus ;

John Donne
47

2. For unto strangers our possession
   Is turn'd, our houses unto aliens gone.

3. Our mothers are become as widows ; we
   As orphans all, and without fathers be,
4. Waters which are our own, we drink and pay ;
   And upon our own wood a price they lay.

5. Our persecutors on our necks do sit ;
   They make us travail, and not intermit ;
6. We stretch our hands unto th' Egyptians
   To get us bread ; and to th' Assyrians.

7. Our fathers did these sins, and are no more ;
   But we do bear the sins they did before.
8. They are but servants, which do rule us thus,
   Yet from their hands none would deliver us.

9. With danger of our life our bread we gat ;
   For in the wilderness the sword did wait.
10. The tempests of this famine we lived in,
    Black as an oven colour'd had our skin.

11. In Judah's cities they the maids abused
    By force, and so women in Sion used.
12. The princes with their hands they hung ; no grace
    Nor honour gave they to the elder's face.

13. Unto the mill our young men carried are,
    And children fell under the wood they bare.
14. Elders the gates, youth did their songs forbear ;
    Gone was our joy ; our dancings, mournings were.

15. Now is the crown fall'n from our head ; and woe
    Be unto us, because we've sinnèd so.
16. For this our hearts do languish, and for this
    Over our eyes a cloudy dimness is.

17. Because Mount Sion desolate doth lie,
     And foxes there do go at liberty ;
18. But Thou, O Lord, art ever, and Thy throne
     From generation to generation.

19. Why shouldst Thou forget us eternally ?
     Or leave us thus long in this misery ?
20. Restore us, Lord, to Thee, that so we may
     Return, and as of old, renew our day.

21. For oughtest Thou, O Lord, despise us thus,
     And to be utterly enraged at us ?

HYMN TO GOD, MY GOD, IN MY SICKNESS

SINCE I am coming to that Holy room,
    Where, with Thy choir of saints for evermore,
I shall be made Thy music ; as I come
    I tune the instrument here at the door,
    And what I must do then, think here before ;

Whilst my physicians by their love are grown
    Cosmographers, and I their map, who lie
Flat on this bed, that by them may be shown
    That this is my south-west discovery,
    Per fretum febris, by these straits to die ;

I joy, that in these straits I see my west ;
    For, though those currents yield return to none,
What shall my west hurt me ?   As west and east
    In all flat maps—and I am one—are one,
    So death doth touch the resurrection.

Is the Pacific sea my home ?   Or are
    The eastern riches ?   Is Jerusalem ?
Anyan, and Magellan, and Gibraltar ?

All straits, and none but straits, are ways to them
Whether where Japhet dwelt, or Cham, or Shem.

We think that Paradise and Calvary,
   Christ's cross and Adam's tree, stood in one place ;
Look, Lord, and find both Adams met in me ;
   As the first Adam's sweat surrounds my face,
   May the last Adam's blood my soul embrace.

So, in His purple wrapp'd, receive me, Lord ;
   By these His thorns, give me His other crown ;
And as to others' souls I preach'd Thy word,
   Be this my text, my sermon to mine own,
     "Therefore that He may raise, the Lord throws
      down."

A HYMN TO GOD THE FATHER

I

WILT Thou forgive that sin where I begun,
   Which was my sin, though it were done before ?
Wilt Thou forgive that sin, through which I run,
   And do run still, though still I do deplore ?
     When Thou hast done, Thou hast not done,
      For I have more.

II

Wilt Thou forgive that sin which I have won
   Others to sin, and made my sin their door ?
Wilt Thou forgive that sin which I did shun
   A year or two, but wallowed in a score ?
     When Thou hast done, Thou hast not done,
      For I have more.

III

I have a sin of fear, that when I have spun
    My last thread, I shall perish on the shore ;
But swear by Thyself, that at my death Thy Son
    Shall shine as he shines now, and heretofore ;
        And, having done that, Thou hast done ;
           I fear no more.

TO GEORGE HERBERT

SENT HIM WITH ONE OF MY SEALS OF THE ANCHOR AND CHRIST

QUI prius assuetus serpentum fasce tabellas
    Signare, hæc nostræ symbola parva domus,
Adscitus domui Domini, patrioque relicto
    Stemmate, nanciscor stemmata jure nova.
Hinc mihi Crux primo quæ fronti impressa lavacro,
    Finibus extensis, anchora facta patet.
Anchoræ in effigiem Crux tandem desinit ipsam,
    Anchora fit tandem Crux tolerata diu.
Hoc tamen ut fiat, Christo vegetatur ab ipso
    Crux, et ab affixo est Anchora facta Jesu.
Nec natalitiis penitus serpentibus orbor,
    Non ita dat Deus, ut auferat ante data.
Qua sapiens, dos est, qua terram lambit et ambit,
    Pestis, at in nostra sit medicina Cruce
Serpens fixa Cruci si sit natura, Crucique
    A fixo nobis gratia tota fluat.
Omnia cum Crux sint, Crux Anchora fixa, sigillum
    Non tam dicendum hoc, quam catechismus erit.
Mitto, nec exigua, exigua sub imagine, dona,
    Pignora amicitiæ, et munera vota preces.
Plura tibi accumulet sanctus cognominis Ille
    Regia qui flavo dona sigillat equo.

A SHEAF OF SNAKES USED HERETOFORE TO BE MY SEAL, THE CREST OF OUR POOR FAMILY

ADOPTED in God's family and so
Our old coat lost, unto new arms I go.
The Cross—my seal at baptism—spread below
Does, by that form, into an Anchor grow.
Crosses grow Anchors ; bear, as thou shouldest do
Thy Cross, and that Cross grows an Anchor too.
But He that makes our Crosses Anchors thus,
Is Christ, who there is crucified for us.
Yet may I, with this, my first serpents hold ;
God gives new blessings, and yet leaves the old ;
The serpent may, as wise, my pattern be ;
My poison, as he feeds on dust, that's me.
And, as he rounds the earth to murder sure,
My death he is, but on the Cross, my cure.
Crucify nature then, and then implore
All grace from Him, crucified there before ;
    Then all is Cross, and that Cross Anchor grown ;
This seal's a catechism, not a seal alone.
Under that little seal great gifts I send,
Works, and prayers, pawns, and fruits of a friend.
And may that saint which rides in our great seal,
To you who bear his name, great bounties deal !

TRANSLATED OUT OF GAZÆUS, "VOTA AMICO FACTA," FOL. 160

GOD grant thee thine own wish, and grant thee mine,
Thou who dost, best friend, in best things outshine ;
May thy soul, ever cheerful, ne'er know cares,
Nor thy life, ever lively, know grey hairs,

Nor thy hand, ever open, know base holds,
Nor thy purse, ever plump, know pleats, or folds,
Nor thy tongue, ever true, know a false thing,
Nor thy word, ever mild, know quarrelling,
Nor thy works, ever equal, know disguise,
Nor thy fame, ever pure, know contumelies,
Nor thy prayers know low objects, still divine ;
God grant thee thine own wish, and grant thee mine.

GEORGE HERBERT

THE CHURCH-PORCH

Perirrhanterium

THOU, whose sweet youth and early hopes inhance
Thy rate and price, and mark thee for a treasure;
Hearken unto a Verser, who may chance
Ryme thee to good, and make a bait of pleasure.
    A verse may finde him, who a sermon flies,
    And turn delight into a sacrifice.

Beware of lust: it doth pollute and foul
Whom God in Baptisme washt with his own blood.
It blots thy lesson written in thy soul;
The holy lines cannot be understood.
    How dare those eyes upon a Bible look,
    Much lesse towards God, whose lust is all their book?

Abstain wholly, or wed. Thy bounteous Lord
Allows thee choise of paths: take no by-wayes;
But gladly welcome what he doth afford;
Not grudging, that thy lust hath bounds and staies.
    Continence hath his joy: weigh both; and so
    If rottennesse have more, let Heaven go.

If God had laid all common, certainly
Man would have been th' incloser: but since now
God hath impal'd us on the contrarie
Man breaks the fence, and every ground will plough.
    O what were man, might he himself misplace
    Sure to be crosse he would shift feet and face.

Drink not the third glasse, which thou canst not tame,
When once it is within thee; but before
Mayst rule it, as thou list; and poure the shame,
Which it would poure on thee, upon the floore.
    It is most just to throw that on the ground,
    Which would throw me there, if I keep the round.

He that is drunken, may his mother kill
Bigge with his sister: he hath lost the reins,
Is outlaw'd by himself: all kinde of ill
Did with his liquour slide into his veins.
    The drunkard forfets Man, and doth devest
    All worldly right, save what he hath by beast.

Shall I, to please anothers wine-sprung minde,
Lose all mine own? God hath giv'n me a measure
Short of his canne, and bodie; must I finde
A pain in that, wherein he findes a pleasure?
    Stay at the third glasse: if thou lose thy hold,
    Then thou are modest, and the wine grows bold.

If reason move not Gallants, quit the room,
(All in a shipwrack shift their severall way)
Let not a common ruine thee intombe:
Be not a beast in courtesie; but stay,
    Stay at the third cup, or forgo the place.
    Wine above all things doth Gods stamp deface.

Yet, if thou sinne in wine or wantonnesse,
Boast not thereof; nor make thy shame thy glorie.
Frailtie gets pardon by submissivenesse;
But he that boasts, shuts that out of his storie.
    He makes flat warre with God, and doth defie
    With his poore clod of earth the spacious sky.

Take not his name, who made thy mouth, in vain:
It gets thee nothing, and hath no excuse.

Lust and wine plead a pleasure, avarice gain :
But the cheap swearer through his open sluce
   Lets his soul runne for nought, as little fearing.
   Were I an *Epicure*, I could bate swearing.

When thou dost tell anothers jest, therein
Omit the oathes, which true wit cannot need :
Pick out of tales the mirth, but not the sinne.
He pares his apple, that will cleanly feed.
   Play not away the vertue of that name,
   Which is thy best stake, when griefs make thee tame.

The cheapest sinnes most dearely punisht are ;
Because to shun them also is so cheap :
For we have wit to mark them, and to spare.
O crumble not away thy souls fair heap.
   If thou wilt die, the gates of hell are broad :
   Pride and full sinnes have made the way a road.

Lie not ; but let thy heart be true to God,
Thy mouth to it, thy actions to them both :
Cowards tell lies, and those that fear the rod ;
The stormie working soul spits lies and froth.
   Dare to be true.   Nothing can need a ly :
   A fault, which needs it most, grows two thereby.

Flie idlenesse, which yet thou canst not flie
By dressing, mistressing, and complement.
If those take up thy day, the sunne will crie
Against thee : for his light was onely lent.
   God gave thy soul brave wings ; put not those feathers
   Into a bed, to sleep out all ill weathers.

Art thou a Magistrate ? then be severe :
If studious ; copie fair, what time hath blurr'd ;
Redeem truth from his jawes : if souldier,
Chase brave employments with a naked sword

Throughout the world.   Fool not : for all may have,
If they dare try, a glorious life, or grave.

O England ! full of sinne, but most of sloth ;
Spit out thy flegme, and fill thy brest with glorie :
Thy Gentrie bleats, as if thy native cloth
Transfus'd a sheepishnesse into thy storie :
    Not that they all are so ; but that the most
    Are gone to grasse, and in the pasture lost.

This losse springs chiefly from our education.
Some till their ground, but let weeds choke their sonne:
Some mark a partridge, never their childes fashion :
Some ship them over, and the thing is done.
    Studie this art, make it thy great designe ;
    And if Gods image move thee not, let thine.

Some great estates provide, but doe not breed
A mast'ring minde ; so both are lost thereby :
Or els they breed them tender, make them need
All that they leave : this is flat povertie.
    For he, that needs five thousand pound to live,
    Is full as poore as he, that needs but five.

The way to make thy sonne rich, is to fill
His minde with rest, before his trunk with riches :
For wealth without contentment, climbes a hill
To feel those tempests, which fly over ditches.
    But if thy sonne can make ten pound his measure,
    Then all thou addest may be call'd his treasure.

When thou dost purpose ought, (within thy power)
Be sure to doe it, though it be but small :
Constancie knits the bones, and makes us stowre,
When wanton pleasures becken us to thrall.
    Who breaks his own bond, forfeiteth himself :
    What nature made a ship, he makes a shelf.

Doe all things like a man, not sneakingly :
Think the king sees thee still ; for his King does.
Simpring is but a lay-hypocrisie :
Give it a corner, and the clue undoes.
　　Who fears to do ill, sets himself to task :
　　Who fears to do well, sure should wear a mask.

Look to thy mouth ; diseases enter there.
Thou hast two sconces, if thy stomack call ;
Carve, or discourse ; do not a famine fear.
Who carves, is kind to two ; who talks, to all.
　　Look on meat, think it dirt, then eat a bit ;
　　And say withall, Earth to earth I commit.

Slight those who say amidst their sickly healths,
Thou liv'st by rule.　What doth not so, but man ?
Houses are built by rule, and common-wealths.
Entice the trusty sunne, if that you can,
　　From his Ecliptick line : becken the skie.
　　Who lives by rule then, keeps good companie.

Who keeps no guard upon himself, is slack,
And rots to nothing at the next great thaw.
Man is a shop of rules, a well truss'd pack,
Whose every parcell under-writes a law.
　　Lose not thy self, nor give thy humours way :
　　God gave them to thee under lock and key.

By all means use sometimes to be alone.
Salute thy self : see what thy soul doth wear.
Dare to look in thy chest ; for 'tis thine own :
And tumble up and down what thou find'st there.
　　Who cannot rest till hee good fellows finde,
　　He breaks up house, turns out of doores his minde.

Be thriftie, but not covetous : therefore give
Thy need, thine honour, and thy friend his due.

Never was scraper brave man.   Get to live ;
Then live, and use it : els, it is not true
    That thou hast gotten.   Surely use alone
    Makes money not a contemptible stone.

Never exceed thy income.   Youth may make
Ev'n with the yeare : but age, if it will hit,
Shoots a bow short, and lessens still his stake,
As the day lessens, and his life with it.
    Thy children, kindred, friends upon thee call ;
    Before thy journey fairly part with all.

Yet in thy thriving still misdoubt some evil ·
Lest gaining gain on thee, and make thee dimme
To all things els.   Wealth is the conjurers devil ;
Whom when he thinks he hath, the devil hath him.
    Gold thou mayst safely touch ; but if it stick
    Unto thy hands, it woundeth to the quick.

What skills it, if a bag of stones or gold
About thy neck do drown thee ? raise thy head ;
Take starres for money ; starres not to be told
By any art, yet to be purchased.
    None is so wastefull as the scraping dame.
    She loseth three for one ; her soul, rest, fame.

By no means runne in debt : take thine own measure.
Who cannot live on twentie pound a yeare,
Cannot on fourtie : he's a man of pleasure,
A kinde of thing that's for it self too deere.
    The curious unthrift makes his cloth too wide,
    And spares himself, but would his taylor chide.

Spend not on hopes.   They that by pleading clothes
Do fortunes seek, when worth and service fail,
Would have their tale beleeved for their oathes,
And are like empty vessels under sail.
    Old courtiers know this ; therefore set out so,
    As all the day thou mayst hold out to go.

In clothes, cheap handsomnesse doth bear the bell.
Wisedome's a trimmer thing, then shop e're gave.
Say not then, This with that lace will do well ;
But, This with my discretion will be brave.
    Much curiousnesse is a perpetuall wooing
    Nothing with labour ; folly long a doing.

Play not for gain, but sport. Who playes for more,
Then he can lose with pleasure, stakes his heart ;
Perhaps his wives too, and whom she hath bore :
Servants and churches also play their part.
    Onely a herauld, who that way doth passe,
    Findes his crackt name at length in the church-glasse.

If yet thou love game at so deere a rate,
Learn this, that hath old gamesters deerely cost :
Dost lose ? rise up : dost winne ? rise in that state.
Who strive to sit out losing hands, are lost.
    Game is a civil gunpowder, in peace
    Blowing up houses with their whole increase.

In conversation boldnesse now bears sway.
But know, that nothing can so foolish be,
As empty boldnesse : therefore first assay
To stuffe thy minde with solid braverie ;
    Then march on gallant : get substantiall worth.
    Boldnesse guilds finely, and will set it forth.

Be sweet to all. Is thy complexion sowre ?
Then keep such companie ; make them thy allay :
Get a sharp wife, a servant that will lowre.
A stumbler stumbles least in rugged way.
    Command thy self in chief. He lifes warre knows,
    Whom all his passions follow, as he goes.

Catch not at quarrels. He that dares not speak
Plainly and home, is coward of the two.
Think not thy fame at ev'ry twitch will break :
By great deeds shew, that thou canst little do ;

And do them not : that shall thy wisdome be ;
And change thy temperance into braverie.

If that thy fame with ev'ry toy be pos'd,
'Tis a thinne webbe, which poysonous fancies make :
But the great souldiers honour was compos'd
Of thicker stuffe, which would endure a shake.
   Wisdome picks friends ; civilitie playes the rest.
   A toy shunn'd cleanly passeth with the best.

Laugh not too much : the wittie man laughs least :
For wit is newes onely to ignorance.
Lesse at thine own things laugh ; lest in the jest
Thy person share, and the conceit advance.
   Make not thy sport, abuses : for the fly
   That feeds on dung, is coloured thereby.

Pick out of mirth, like stones out of thy ground,
Profanenesse, filthinesse, abusivenesse.
These are the scumme, with which course wits abound :
The fine may spare these well, yet not go lesse.
   All things are bigge with jest : nothing that's plain,
   But may be wittie, if thou hast the vein.

Wit's an unruly engine, wildly striking
Sometimes a friend, sometimes the engineer.
Hast thou the knack ? pamper it not with liking :
But if thou want it, buy it not too deere.
   Many affecting wit beyond their power,
   Have got to be a deare fool for an houre.

A sad wise valour is the brave complexion,
That leads the van, and swallows up the cities.
The gigler is a milk-maid, whom infection,
Or a fir'd beacon frighteth from his ditties.
   Then he's the sport : the mirth then in him rests,
   And the sad man is cock of all his jests.

Towards great persons use respective boldnesse :
That temper gives them theirs, and yet doth take
Nothing from thine : in service, care, or coldnesse
Doth ratably thy fortunes marre or make.
　　Feed no man in his sinnes : for adulation
　　Doth make thee parcell-devil in damnation.

Envie not greatnesse : for thou mak'st thereby
Thy self the worse, and so the distance greater.
Be not thine own worm : yet such jealousie,
As hurts not others, but may make thee better,
　　Is a good spurre.　Correct thy passions spite ;
　　Then may the beasts draw thee to happy light.

When basenesse is exalted, do not bate
The place its honour, for the persons sake.
The shrine is that which thou dost venerate ;
And not the beast, that bears it on his back.
　　I care not though the cloth of state should be
　　Not of rich arras, but mean tapestrie.

Thy friend put in thy bosome : wear his eies
Still in thy heart, that he may see what's there.
If cause require, thou art his sacrifice ;
Thy drops of bloud must pay down all his fear :
　　But love is lost ; the way of friendship's gone,
　　Though *David* had his *Jonathan, Christ* his *John.*

Yet be not surety, if thou be a father.
Love is a personall debt.　I cannot give
My childrens right, nor ought he take it : rather
Both friends should die, then hinder them to live.
　　Fathers first enter bonds to natures ends ;
　　And are her sureties, ere they are a friends.

If thou be single, all thy goods and ground
Submit to love ; but yet not more then all.
Give one estate, as one life.　None is bound
To work for two, who brought himself to thrall.

God made me one man ; love makes me no more,
Till labour come, and make my weaknesse score.

In thy discourse, if thou desire to please :
All such is courteous, usefull, new, or wittie.
Usefulnesse comes by labour, wit by ease ;
Courtesie grows in court ; news in the citie.
    Get a good stock of these, then draw the card ;
    That suites him best, of whom thy speech is heard.

Entice all neatly to what they know best ;
For so thou dost thy self and him a pleasure :
(But a proud ignorance will lose his rest,
Rather than shew his cards) steal from his treasure
    What to ask further.   Doubts well rais'd do lock
    The speaker to thee, and preserve thy stock.

If thou be Master-gunner, spend not all
That thou canst speak, at once ; but husband it,
And give men turns of speech : do not forestall
By lavishnesse thine own, and others wit,
    As if thou mad'st thy will.   A civil guest
    Will no more talk all, then eat all the feast.

Be calm in arguing : for fiercenesse makes
Errour a fault, and truth discourtesie.
Why should I feel another mans mistakes
More, then his sicknesses or povertie ?
    In love I should : but anger is not love,
    Nor wisdome neither : therefore gently move.

Calmnesse is great advantage : he that lets
Another chafe, may warm him at his fire :
Mark all his wandrings, and enjoy his frets ;
As cunning fencers suffer heat to tire.
    Truth dwels not in the clouds : the bow that's there,
    Doth often aim at, never hit the sphere.

Mark what another sayes : for many are
Full of themselves, and answer their own notion.
Take all into thee ; then with equall care
Ballance each dramme of reason, like a potion.
  If truth be with thy friend, be with them both :
  Share in the conquest, and confesse a troth.

Be usefull where thou livest, that they may
Both want, and wish thy pleasing presence still.
Kindnesse, good parts, great places are the way
To compasse this.   Finde out mens wants and will,
  And meet them there.   All worldly joyes go lesse
  To the one joy of doing kindnesses.

Pitch thy behaviour low, thy projects high ;
So shalt thou humble and magnanimous be :
Sink not in spirit : who aimeth at the sky,
Shoots higher much then he that means a tree.
  A grain of glorie mixt with humblenesse
  Cures both a fever and lethargicknesse.

Let thy minde still be bent, still plotting where,
And when, and how the businesse may be done.
Slacknesse breeds worms ; but the sure traveller,
Though he alight sometimes, still goeth on.
  Active and stirring spirits live alone.
  Write on the others, Here lies such a one.

Slight not the smallest losse, whether it be
In love or honour : take account of all ;
Shine like the sunne in every corner : see
Whether thy stock of credit swell, or fall.
  Who say, I care not, those I give for lost ;
  And to instruct them, 'twill not quit the cost.

Scorn no mans love, though of a mean degree ;
(Love is a present for a mightie king)
Much lesse make any one thine enemie.
As gunnes destroy, so may a little sling.

The cunning workman never doth refuse
The meanest tool, that he may chance to use.

All forrain wisdome doth amount to this,
To take all that is given ; whether wealth,
Or love, or language ; nothing comes amisse ;
A good digestion turneth all to health :
    And then as farre as fair behaviour may,
    Strike off all scores ; none are so cleare as they.

Keep all thy native good, and naturalize
All forrain of that name ; but scorn their ill :
Embrace their activenesse, not vanities.
Who follows all things, forfeiteth his will.
    If thou observest strangers in each fit,
    In time they'l runne thee out of all thy wit.

Affect in things about thee cleanlinesse,
That all may gladly board thee, as a flowre.
Slovens take up their stock of noisomnesse
Beforehand, and anticipate their last houre.
    Let thy mindes sweetnesse have his operation
    Upon thy body, clothes, and habitation.

In Almes regard thy means, and others merit.
Think heav'n a better bargain, then to give
Onely thy single market-money for it.
Joyn hands with God to make a man to live.
    Give to all something ; to a good poore man,
    Till thou change names, and be where he began.

Man is Gods image ; but a poore man is
Christs stamp to boot : both images regard.
God reckons for him, counts the favour his :
Write, So much giv'n to God ; thou shalt be heard.
    Let thy almes go before, and keep heav'ns gate
    Open for thee ; or both may come too late.

Restore to God his due in tithe and time :
A tithe purloin'd cankers the whole estate.
Sundaies observe : think when the bells do chime,
'Tis angels musick ; therefore come not late.
    God then deals blessings : If a king did so,
     Who would not haste, nay give, to see the show ?

Twice on the day his due is understood ;
For all the week thy food so oft he gave thee.
Thy cheere is mended ; bate not of the food,
Because 'tis better, and perhaps may save thee.
    Thwart not th' Almighty God : O be not crosse.
    Fast when thou wilt ; but then 'tis gain, not losse.

Though private prayer be a brave designe,
Yet publick hath more promises, more love :
And love's a weight to hearts, to eies a signe.
We all are but cold suitours ; let us move
    Where it is warmest. Leave thy six and seven ;
    Pray with the most : for where most pray, is heaven.

When once thy foot enters the church, be bare.
God is more there, then thou : for thou art there
Onely by his permission. Then beware,
And make thy self all reverence and fear.
    Kneeling ne're spoil'd silk stocking : quit thy state.
    All equall are within the churches gate.

Resort to sermons, but to prayers most :
Praying 's the end of preaching. O be drest ;
Stay not for th' other pin : why thou hast lost
A joy for it worth worlds. Thus hell doth jest
    Away thy blessings, and extreamly flout thee,
    Thy clothes being fast, but thy soul loose about thee.

In time of service seal up both thine eies,
And send them to thine heart ; that spying sinne,
They may weep out the stains by them did rise :
Those doores being shut, all by the eare comes in.

Who marks in church-time others symmetrie,
Makes all their beautie his deformitie.

Let vain or busie thoughts have there no part :
Bring not thy plough, thy plots, thy pleasures thither.
Christ purg'd his temple ; so must thou thy heart.
All worldly thoughts are but theeves met together
    To couzin thee.   Look to thy actions well :
    For churches are either our heav'n or hell.

Judge not the preacher ; for he is thy Judge :
If thou mislike him, thou conceiv'st him not.
God calleth preaching folly.   Do not grudge
To pick out treasures from an earthen pot.
    The worst speak something good : if all want sense,
    God takes a text, and preacheth patience.

He that gets patience, and the blessing which
Preachers conclude with, hath not lost his pains.
He that by being at church escapes the ditch,
Which he might fall in by companions, gains.
    He that loves Gods abode, and to combine
    With saints on earth, shall one day with them shine.

Jest not at preachers language, or expression :
How know'st thou, but thy sinnes made him miscarrie ?
Then turn thy faults and his into confession :
God sent him, whatsoe're he be : O tarry,
    And love him for his Master : his condition,
    Though it be ill, makes him no ill Physician.

None shall in hell such bitter pangs endure,
As those, who mock at Gods way of salvation.
Whom oil and balsames kill, what salve can cure ?
They drink with greedinesse a full damnation.
    The Jews refused thunder ; and we, folly.
    Though God do hedge us in, yet who is holy ?

Summe up at night, what thou hast done by day ;
And in the morning, what thou hast to do.
Dresse and undresse thy soul : mark the decay
And growth of it : if with thy watch, that too
   Be down, then winde up both, since we shall be
   Most surely judg'd, make thy accounts agree.

In brief, acquit thee bravely ; play the man.
Look not on pleasures as they come, but go.
Deferre not the least vertue : lifes poore span
Make not an ell, by trifling in thy wo.
   If thou do ill ; the joy fades, not the pains :
   If well ; the pain doth fade, the joy remains.

REDEMPTION

HAVING been tenant long to a rich Lord,
   Not thriving, I resolved to be bold,
   And make a suit unto him, to afford
A new small-rented lease, and cancell th' old.

In heaven at his manour I him sought :
   They told me there, that he was lately gone
   About some land, which he had dearly bought
Long since on earth, to take possession.

I straight return'd, and knowing his great birth,
   Sought him accordingly in great resorts ;
   In cities, theatres, gardens, parks, and courts :
At length I heard a ragged noise and mirth

   Of theeves and murderers : there I him espied,
   Who straight, *Your suit is granted*, said, and died.

EASTER

Rise heart ; thy Lord is risen.   Sing his praise
                    Without delayes,
Who takes thee by the hand, that thou likewise
                    With him mayst rise :
That, as his death calcined thee to dust,
His life may make thee gold, and much more just.

Awake, my lute, and struggle for thy part
                    With all thy art.
The crosse taught all wood to resound his name,
                    Who bore the same.
His streched sinews taught all strings, what key
Is best to celebrate this most high day.

Consort both heart and lute, and twist a song
                    Pleasant and long :
Or since all musick is but three parts vied
                    And multiplied ;
O let thy blessed Spirit bear a part,
And make up our defects with his sweet art.

I got me flowers to straw thy way ;
I got me boughs off many a tree :
But thou wast up by break of day,
And brought'st thy sweets along with thee.

The Sunne arising in the East,
Though he give light, & th' East perfume ;
If they should offer to contest
With thy arising, they presume.

Can there be any day but this,
Though many sunnes to shine endeavour ?
We count three hundred, but we misse :
There is but one, and that one ever.

H. BAPTISME

Since, Lord, to thee
A narrow way and little gate
Is all the passage, on my infancie
Thou didst lay hold, and antedate
My faith in me.

O let me still
Write thee great God, and me a childe :
Let me be soft and supple to thy will,
Small to my self, to others milde,
Behither ill.

Although by stealth
My flesh get on, yet let her sister
My soul bid nothing, but preserve her wealth :
The growth of flesh is but a blister ;
Childhood is health.

SINNE

Lord, with what care hast thou begirt us round !
  Parents first season us : then schoolmasters
  Deliver us to laws ; they send us bound
To rules of reason, holy messengers,

Pulpits and sundayes, sorrow dogging sinne,
  Afflictions sorted, anguish of all sizes,
  Fine nets and stratagems to catch us in,
Bibles laid open, millions of surprises,

Blessings beforehand, tyes of gratefulnesse,
    The sound of glorie ringing in our eares :
    Without, our shame ; within, our consciences ;
Angels and grace, eternall hopes and fears.

    Yet all these fences and their whole aray
    One cunning bosome-sinne blows quite away.

AFFLICTION

When first thou didst entice to thee my heart,
                I thought the service brave.
So many joyes I writ down for my part,
                Besides what I might have
Out of my stock of naturall delights,
Augmented with thy gracious benefits.

I looked on thy furniture so fine,
                And made it fine to me :
Thy glorious household-stuffe did me entwine,
                And 'tice me unto thee.
Such starres I counted mine : both heav'n and earth
Payd me my wages in a world of mirth.

What pleasures could I want, whose King I served ?
                Where joyes my fellows were.
Thus argu'd into hopes, my thoughts reserved
                No place for grief or fear.
Therefore my sudden soul caught at the place,
And made her youth and fiercenesse seek thy face.

At first thou gav'st me milk and sweetnesses ;
                I had my wish and way :
My dayes were straw'd with flow'rs and happinesse ;
                There was no moneth but May.
But with my yeares sorrow did twist and grow,
And made a partie unawares for wo.

My flesh began unto my soul in pain,
                Sicknesses cleave my bones ;
Consuming agues dwell in ev'ry vein,
                And tune my breath to grones.
Sorrow was all my soul ; I scarce beleeved,
Till grief did tell me roundly, that I lived.

When I got health, thou took'st away my life,
                And more ; for my friends die :
My mirth and age was lost ; a blunted knife
                Was of more use then I.
Thus thinne and lean without a fence or friend,
I was blown through with ev'ry storm and winde.

Whereas my birth and spirit rather took
                The way that takes the town ;
Thou didst betray me to a lingring book,
                And wrap me in a gown.
I was entangled in the world of strife,
Before I had the power to change my life.

Yet, for I threatned oft the siege to raise,
                Not simpring all mine age,
Thou often didst with Academick praise
                Melt and dissolve my rage.
I took thy sweetned pill, till I came neare ;
I could not go away, nor persevere.

Yet lest perchance I should too happie be
                In my unhappinesse,
Turning my purge to food, thou throwest me
                Into more sicknesses.
Thus doth thy power crosse-bias me, not making
Thine own gift good, yet me from my wayes taking.

Now I am here, what thou wilt do with me
                None of my books will show :
I reade, and sigh, and wish I were a tree ;
                For sure then I should grow

To fruit or shade : at least some bird would trust
Her household to me, and I should be just.

Yet, though thou troublest me, I must be meek ;
                 In weaknesse must be stout.
Well, I will change the service, and go seek
                 Some other master out.
Ah my deare God ! though I am clean forgot,
Let me not love thee, if I love thee not.

REPENTANCE

LORD, I confesse my sinne is great ;
  Great is my sinne.   Oh ! gently treat
With thy quick flow'r, thy momentanie bloom ;
               Whose life still pressing
               Is one undressing,
  A steadie aiming at a tombe.

Mans age is two houres work, or three :
  Each day doth round about us see.
Thus are we to delights : but we are all
               To sorrows old,
               If life be told
From what life feeleth, Adams fall.

O let thy height of mercie then
  Compassionate short-breathed men.
Cut me not off for my most foul transgression :
               I do confesse
               My foolishnesse ;
  My God, accept of my confession.

Sweeten at length this bitter bowl,
  Which thou hast pour'd into my soul ;

Thy wormwood turn to health, windes to fair weather :
> For if thou stay,
> I and this day,
As we did rise, we die together.

When thou for sinne rebukest man,
Forthwith he waxeth wo and wan :
Bitternesse fills our bowels ; all our hearts
> Pine, and decay,
> And drop away,
And carrie with them th' other parts.

But thou wilt sinne and grief destroy ;
That so the broken bones may joy,
And tune together in a well-set song,
> Full of his praises,
> Who dead men raises.
Fractures well cur'd make us more strong.

PRAYER

PRAYER the Churches banquet, Angels age,
> Gods breath in man returning to his birth,
> The soul in paraphrase, heart in pilgrimage,
The Christian plummet sounding heav'n and earth ;

Engine against th' Almightie, sinners towre,
> Reversed thunder, Christ-side-piercing spear,
> The six-daies—world transposing in an houre,
A kinde of tune, which all things heare and fear ;

Softnesse, and peace, and joy, and love, and blisse,
> Exalted Manna, gladnesse of the best,
> Heaven in ordinarie, man well drest,
The milkie may, the bird of Paradise,
> Church-bels beyond the starres heard, the souls bloud,
> The land of spices ; something understood.

LOVE

I

IMMORTALL Love, authour of this great frame,
    Sprung from that beautie which can never fade ;
    How hath man parcel'd out thy glorious name,
And thrown it on that dust which thou hast made,

While mortall love doth all the title gain !
    Which siding with invention, they together
    Bear all the sway, possessing heart and brain,
(Thy workmanship) and give thee share in neither.

Wit fancies beautie, beautie raiseth wit :
    The world is theirs ; they two play out the game,
    Thou standing by : and though thy glorious name
Wrought out deliverance from th' infernall pit,

    Who sings thy praise ? onely a skarf or glove
    Doth warm our hands, and make them write of love.

II

IMMORTALL Heat, O let thy greater flame
    Attract the lesser to it : let those fires,
    Which shall consume the world, first make it tame ;
And kindle in our hearts such true desires,

As may consume our lusts, and make thee way.
    Then shall our hearts pant thee ; then shall our
        brain
    All her invention on thine Altar lay,
And there in hymnes send back thy fire again :

Our eies shall see thee, which before saw dust ;
    Dust blown by wit, till that they both were blinde :
    Thou shalt recover all thy goods in kinde,
Who wert disseized by usurping lust :

    All knees shall bow to thee ; all wits shall rise,
    And praise him who did make and mend our eies.

THE TEMPER

How should I praise thee, Lord ! how should my rymes
    Gladly engrave thy love in steel,
    If what my soul doth feel sometimes,
       My soul might ever feel !

Although there were some fourtie heav'ns, or more,
    Sometimes I peere above them all ;
    Sometimes I hardly reach a score,
       Sometimes to hell I fall.

O rack me not to such a vast extent ;
    Those distances belong to thee :
    The world's too little for thy tent,
       A grave too big for me.

Wilt thou meet arms with man, that thou dost stretch
    A crumme of dust from heav'n to hell ?
    Will great God measure with a wretch ?
       Shall he thy stature spell ?

O let me, when thy roof my soul hath hid,
    O let me roost and nestle there :
    Then of a sinner thou art rid,
       And I of hope and fear.

Yet take thy way ; for sure thy way is best :
    Stretch or contract me thy poore debter :
    This is but tuning of my breast,
        To make the musick better.

Whether I flie with angels, fall with dust,
    Thy hands made both, and I am there :
    Thy power and love, my love and trust
        Make one place ev'ry where.

JORDAN

Who sayes that fictions onely and false hair
Become a verse ?   Is there in truth no beautie ?
Is all good structure in a winding stair ?
May no lines passe, except they do their dutie
    Not to a true, but painted chair ?

Is it no verse, except enchanted groves
And sudden arbours shadow course-spunne lines ?
Must purling streams refresh a lovers loves ?
Must all be vail'd, while he that reades, divines,
    Catching the sense at two removes ?

Shepherds are honest people ; let them sing :
Riddle who list, for me, and pull for Prime :
I envie no mans nightingale or spring ;
Nor let them punish me with losse of ryme,
    Who plainly say, *My God, My King.*

GRACE

    My stock lies dead, and no increase
    Doth my dull husbandrie improve :
    O let thy graces without cease
           Drop from above !

If still the sunne should hide his face,
Thy house would but a dungeon prove,
Thy works nights captives : O let grace
       Drop from above !

The dew doth ev'ry morning fall ;
And shall the dew out-strip thy dove ?
The dew, for which grasse cannot call,
       Drop from above.

Death is still working like a mole,
And digs my grave at each remove :
Let grace work too, and on my soul
       Drop from above.

Sinne is still hammering my heart
Unto a hardnesse, void of love :
Let suppling grace, to crosse his art,
       Drop from above.

O come ! for thou dost know the way.
Or if to me thou wilt not move,
Remove me, where I need not say,
       Drop from above.

MATTENS

I CANNOT ope mine eyes,
But thou art ready there to catch
My morning-soul and sacrifice :
Then we must needs for that day make a match.

My God, what is a heart ?
Silver, or gold, or precious stone,
Or starre, or rainbow, or a part
Of all these things, or all of them in one ?

My God, what is a heart,
That thou shouldst it so eye, and wooe,
Powring upon it all thy art,
As if that thou hadst nothing els to do?

Indeed mans whole estate
Amounts (and richly) to serve thee:
He did not heav'n and earth create,
Yet studies them, not him by whom they be.

Teach me thy love to know;
That this new light, which now I see,
May both the work and workmen show:
Then by a sunne-beam I will climbe to thee.

SINNE

O THAT I could a sinne once see!
We paint the devil foul, yet he
Hath some good in him, all agree.
Sinne is flat opposite to th' Almighty, seeing
It wants the good of *vertue*, and of *being*.

But God more care of us hath had:
If apparitions make us sad,
By sight of sinne we should grow mad.
Yet as in sleep we see foul death, and live:
So devils are our sinnes in perspective.

CONTENT

PEACE mutt'ring thoughts, and do not grudge to keep
Within the walls of your own breast:
Who cannot on his own bed sweetly sleep,
Can on anothers hardly rest.

Gad not abroad at ev'ry quest and call
    Of an untrained hope or passion.
To court each place or fortune that doth fall,
    Is wantonnesse in contemplation.

Mark how the fire in flints doth quiet lie,
    Content and warm t' it self alone :
But when it would appeare to others eye,
    Without a knock it never shone.

Give me the pliant minde, whose gentle measure
    Complies and suits with all estates ;
Which can let loose to a crown, and yet with pleasure
    Take up within a cloisters gates.

This soul doth span the world, and hang content
    From either pole unto the centre :
Where in each room of the well-furnisht tent
    He lies warm, and without adventure.

The brags of life are but a nine dayes wonder ;
    And after death the fumes that spring
From private bodies, make as big a thunder,
    As those which rise from a huge King.

Onely thy Chronicle is lost ; and yet
    Better by worms be all once spent,
Then to have hellish moths still gnaw and fret
    Thy name in books, which may not rent :

When all thy deeds, whose brunt thou feel'st alone,
    Are chaw'd by others pens and tongues ;
And as their wit is, their digestion,
    Thy nourisht fame is weak or strong.

Then cease discoursing soul, till thine own ground,
    Do not thy self or friends importune.
He that by seeking hath himself once found,
    Hath euer found a happie fortune.

CONSTANCIE

WHO is the honest man ?
He that doth still and strongly good pursue,
To God, his neighbour, and himself most true :
    Whom neither force nor fawning can
Unpinne, or wrench from giving all their due.

    Whose honestie is not
So loose or easie, that a ruffling winde
Can blow away, or glittering look it blinde :
    Who rides his sure and even trot,
While the world now rides by, now lags behinde.

    Who, when great trials come,
Nor seeks, nor shunnes them ; but doth calmly stay
Till he the thing and the example weigh :
    All being brought into a summe,
What place or person calls for, he doth pay.

    Whom none can work or wooe
To use in any thing a trick or sleight,
For above all things he abhorres deceit :
    His words and works and fashion too
All of a piece, and all are cleare and straight.

    Who never melts or thaws
At close tentations : when the day is done,
His goodnesse sets not, but in dark can runne :
    The sunne to others writeth laws,
And is their vertue ; Vertue is his Sunne.

    Who, when he is to treat
With sick folks, women, those whom passions sway,
Allows for that, and keeps his constant way :
    Whom others faults do not defeat ;
But though men fail him, yet his part doth play.

Whom nothing can procure,
When the wide world runnes bias, from his will
To writhe his limbes, and share, not mend the ill.
This is the Mark-man, safe and sure,
Who still is right, and prayes to be so still.

VERTUE

SWEET day, so cool, so calm, so bright,
The bridall of the earth and skie :
The dew shall weep thy fall to night ;
        For thou must die.

Sweet rose, whose hue angrie and brave
Bids the rash gazer wipe his eye :
Thy root is ever in its grave,
        And thou must die.

Sweet spring, full of sweet dayes and roses,
A box where sweets compacted lie ;
My musick shows ye have your closes,
        And all must die.

Onely a sweet and vertuous soul,
Like season'd timber, never gives ;
But though the whole world turn to coal,
        Then chiefly lives.

LIFE

I MADE a posie, while the day ran by :
Here will I smell my remnant out, and tie
        My life within this band.

But time did becken to the flowers, and they
By noon most cunningly did steal away,
             And wither'd in my hand.

My hand was next to them, and then my heart :
I took, without more thinking, in good part
             Times gentle admonition :
Who did so sweetly deaths sad taste convey,
Making my minde to smell my fatall day ;
             Yet sugring the suspicion.

Farewell deare flowers, sweetly your time ye spent,
Fit, while ye liv'd, for smell or ornament,
             And after death for cures
I follow straight without complaints or grief,
Since if my scent be good, I care not, if
             It be as short as yours.

MORTIFICATION

How soon doth man decay !
When clothes are taken from a chest of sweets
      To swaddle infants, whose young breath
          Scarce knows the way ;
    Those clouts are little winding sheets,
Which do consigne and send them unto death.

When boyes go first to bed,
They step into their voluntarie graves,
      Sleep bindes them fast ; onely their breath
          Makes them not dead :
    Successive nights, like rolling waves,
Convey them quickly, who are bound for death.

When youth is frank and free,
And calls for musick, while his veins do swell,
      All day exchanging mirth and breath
          In companie ;

That musick summons to the knell,
Which shall befriend him at the house of death.

When man grows staid and wise,
Getting a house and home, where he may move
Within the circle of his breath,
Schooling his eyes ;
That dumbe inclosure maketh love
Unto the coffin, that attends his death.

When age grows low and weak,
Marking his grave, and thawing ev'ry yeare,
Till all do melt, and drown his breath
When he would speak ;
A chair or litter shows the biere,
Which shall convey him to the house of death.

Man, ere he is aware,
Hath put together a solemnitie,
And drest his herse, while he has breath
As yet to spare :
Yet Lord, instruct us so to die,
That all these dyings may be life in death.

MISERIE

LORD, let the Angels praise thy name.
Man is a foolish thing, a foolish thing,
Folly and Sinne play all his game.
His house still burns, and yet he still doth sing,
Man is but grasse,
He knows it, fill the glasse.

How canst thou brook his foolishnesse ?
Why he'l not lose a cup of drink for thee :
Bid him but temper his excesse ;

Not he : he knows, where he can better be,
        As he will swear,
        Then to serve thee in fear.

What strange pollutions doth he wed,
And make his own ? as if none knew, but he.
No man shall beat into his head,
That thou within his curtains drawn canst see :
        They are of cloth,
        Where never yet came moth.

The best of men, turn but thy hand
For one poore minute, stumble at a pinne :
    They would not have their actions scann'd,
Nor any sorrow tell them that they sinne,
        Though it be small,
        And measure not their fall.

They quarrell thee, and would give over
The bargain made to serve thee : but thy love
    Holds them unto it, and doth cover
Their follies with the wing of thy milde Dove,
        Not suff'ring those
        Who would, to be thy foes.

My God, Man cannot praise thy name :
Thou art all brightnesse, perfect puritie ;
    The sunne holds down his head for shame,
Dead with eclipses, when we speak of thee :
        How shall infection
        Presume on thy perfection ?

As dirtie hands foul all they touch,
And those things most, which are most pure and fine :
    So our clay hearts, ev'n when we crouch
To sing thy praises, make them lesse divine.
        Yet either this,
        Or none thy portion is.

Man cannot serve thee ; let him go,
And serve the swine : there, there is his delight :
   He doth not like this vertue, no ;
Give him his dirt to wallow in all night :
      These Preachers make
      His head to shoot and ake.

Oh foolish man ! where are thine eyes ?
How hast thou lost them in a croud of cares ?
   Thou pull'st the rug, and wilt not rise,
No not to purchase the whole pack of starres :
      There let them shine,
      Thou must go sleep, or dine.

The bird that sees a daintie bowre
Made in the tree, where she was wont to sit,
   Wonders and sings, but not his power
Who made the arbour : this exceeds her wit.
      But Man doth know
      The spring, whence all things flow :

And yet as though he knew it not,
His knowledge winks, and lets his humours reigne ;
   They make his life a constant blot,
And all the bloud of God to run in vain.
      Ah wretch ! what verse
      Can thy strange wayes rehearse ?

Indeed at first Man was a treasure,
A box of jewels, shop of rarities,
   A ring, whose posie was, *My pleasure :*
He was a garden in a Paradise :
      Glorie and grace
      Did crown his heart and face.

But sinne hath fool'd him.   Now he is
A lump of flesh, without a foot or wing
   To raise him to the glimpse of blisse :

A sick toss'd vessel, dashing on each thing ;
              Nay, his own shelf :
              My God, I mean my self.

JORDAN

WHEN first my lines of heav'nly joyes made mention,
Such was their lustre, they did so excell,
That I sought out quaint words, and trim invention ;
My thoughts began to burnish, sprout, and swell.
Curling with metaphors a plain intention,
Decking the sense, as if it were to sell.

Thousands of notions in my brain did runne,
Off'ring their service, if I were not sped :
I often blotted what I had begunne ;
This was not quick enough, and that was dead.
Nothing could seem too rich to clothe the sunne,
Much lesse those joyes which trample on his head.

As flames do work and winde, when they ascend,
So did I weave my self into the sense.
But while I bustled, I might heare a friend
Whisper, *How wide is all this long pretence !*
There is in love a sweetnesse readie penn'd :
Copie out onely that, and save expense.

THE BRITISH CHURCH

I JOY, deare Mother, when I view
Thy perfect lineaments, and hue
              Both sweet and bright.

Beautie in thee takes up her place,
And dates her letters from thy face,
              When she doth write.

A fine aspect in fit aray,
Neither too mean, nor yet too gay,
        Shows who is best.

Outlandish looks may not compare :
For all they either painted are,
        Or else undrest.

She on the hills, which wantonly
Allureth all, in hope to be
        By her preferr'd,

Hath kiss'd so long her painted shrines,
That ev'n her face by kissing shines,
        For her reward.

She in the valley is so shie
Of dressing, that her hair doth lie
        About her eares :

While she avoids her neighbours pride,
She wholly goes on th' other side,
        And nothing wears.

But dearest Mother, (what those misse)
The mean thy praise and glorie is,
        And long may be.

Blessed be God, whose love it was
To double-moat thee with his grace,
        And none but thee.

THE QUIP

THE merrie world did on a day
With his train-bands and mates agree
To meet together, where I lay,
And all in sport to geere at me.

First, Beautie crept into a rose,
Which when I pluckt not, Sir, said she,
Tell me, I pray, Whose hands are those ?
But thou shalt answer, Lord, for me.

Then Money came, and chinking still,
What tune is this, poore man ? said he :
I heard in Musick you had skill.
But thou shalt answer, Lord, for me.

Then came brave Glorie puffing by
In silks that whistled, who but he ?
He scarce allow'd me half an eie,
But thou shalt answer, Lord, for me.

Then came quick Wit and Conversation,
And he would needs a comfort be,
And, to be short, make an oration.
But thou shalt answer, Lord, for me.

Yet when the houre of thy designe
To answer these fine things shall come ;
Speak not at large, say, I am thine :
And then they have their answer home.

DULNESSE

WHY do I languish thus, drooping and dull,
            As if I were all earth ?
O give me quicknesse, that I may with mirth
            Praise thee brim-full !

The wanton lover in a curious strain
            Can praise his fairest fair ;
And with quaint metaphors her curled hair
            Curl o're again.

Thou art my lovelinesse, my life, my light,
      Beautie alone to me :
Thy bloudy death and undeserv'd, makes thee
      Pure red and white.

When all perfections as but one appeare,
      That those thy form doth show,
The very dust, where thou dost tread and go,
      Makes beauties here ;

Where are my lines then ? my approaches ? views ?
      Where are my window-songs ?
Lovers are still pretending, & ev'n wrongs
      Sharpen their Muse :

But I am lost in flesh, whose sugred lyes
      Still mock me, and grow bold :
Sure thou didst put a minde there, if I could
      Finde where it lies.

Lord, cleare thy gift, that with a constant wit
      I may but look towards thee :
Look onely ; for to *love* thee, who can be,
      What angel fit ?

TIME

MEETING with Time, slack thing, said I,
Thy sithe is dull ; whet it for shame.
No marvell, Sir, he did replie,
If it at length deserve some blame :
    But where one man would have me grinde it,
    Twentie for one too sharp do finde it.

Perhaps some such of old did passe,
Who above all things lov'd this life ;
To whom thy sithe a hatchet was,
Which now is but a pruning knife.
    Christs coming hath made man thy debter,
    Since by thy cutting he grows better.

And in his blessing thou art blest :
For where thou onely wert before
An executioner at best ;
Thou art a gard'ner now, and more,
    An usher to convey our souls
    Beyond the utmost starres and poles.

And this is that makes life so long,
While it detains us from our God.
Ev'n pleasures here increase the wrong,
And length of dayes lengthen the rod.
    Who wants the place, where God doth dwell,
    Partakes already half of hell.

Of what strange length must that needs be,
Which ev'n eternitie excludes !
Thus farre Time heard me patiently :
Then chafing said, This man deludes :
    What do I here before his doore ?
    He doth not crave lesse time, but more.

GRATEFULNESSE

Thou that hast giv'n so much to me,
Give one thing more, a gratefull heart.
See how thy beggar works on thee
                    By art.

He makes thy gifts occasion more,
And sayes, If he in this be crost,
All thou hast giv'n him heretofore
        Is lost.

But thou didst reckon, when at first
Thy word our hearts and hands did crave,
What it would come to at the worst
        To save.

Perpetuall knockings at thy doore,
Tears sullying thy transparent rooms,
Gift upon gift, much would have more,
        And comes.

This not withstanding, thou wentst on,
And didst allow us all our noise :
Nay thou hast made a sigh and grone
        Thy joyes.

Not that thou hast not still above
Much better tunes, then grones can make ;
But that these countrey-aires thy love
        Did take.

Wherefore I crie, and crie again ;
And in no quiet canst thou be,
Till I a thankfull heart obtain
        Of thee :

Not thankfull, when it pleaseth me ;
As if thy blessings had spare dayes :
But such a heart, whose pulse may be
        Thy praise.

GIDDINESSE

Oh, what a thing is man ! how farre from power,
    From setled peace and rest !
He is some twentie sev'rall men at least
    Each sev'rall houre.

One while he counts of heav'n, as of his treasure:
    But then a thought creeps in,
And calls him coward, who for fear of sinne
    Will lose a pleasure.

Now he will fight it out, and to the warres ;
    Now eat his bread in peace,
And snudge in quiet : now he scorns increase ;
    Now all day spares.

He builds a house, which quickly down must go,
    As if a whirlwinde blew
And crusht the building : and it's partly true,
    His minde is so.

O what a sight were Man, if his attires
    Did alter with his minde ;
And like a Dolphins skinne, his clothes combin'd
    With his desires !

Surely if each one saw anothers heart,
    There would be no commerce,
No sale or bargain passe : all would disperse,
    And live apart.

Lord, mend or rather make us ; one creation
    Will not suffice our turn :
Except thou make us dayly, we shall spurn
    Our own salvation.

THE COLLAR

I STRUCK the board, and cry'd, No more.
　　　　I will abroad.
What ? shall I ever sigh and pine ?
My lines and life are free ; free as the rode,
　　Loose as the winde, as large as store.
　　　　Shall I be still in suit ?
　　Have I no harvest but a thorn
　　To let me bloud, and not restore
What I have lost with cordiall fruit ?
　　　　　　Sure there was wine
　　Before my sighs did drie it : there was corn
　　　Before my tears did drown it.
　　Is the yeare onely lost to me ?
　　　Have I no bayes to crown it ?
No flowers, no garlands gay ? all blasted ?
　　　　All wasted ?
　　Not so, my heart : but there is fruit,
　　　　And thou hast hands.
　　Recover all thy sigh-blown age
On double pleasures : leave thy cold dispute
Of what is fit, and not forsake thy cage,
　　　　Thy rope of sands,
Which pettie thoughts have made, and made to thee
　　Good cable, to enforce and draw,
　　　　And be thy law,
While thou didst wink and wouldst not see.
　　　　Away ; take heed :
　　　　I will abroad.
Call in thy deaths head there ; tie up thy fears.
　　　　He that forbears
　　To suit and serve his need,
　　　　Deserves his load.
But as I rav'd and grew more fierce and wilde
　　　　At every word,

Me thoughts I heard one calling, *Childe* :
                    And I reply'd, *My Lord.*

THE GLIMPSE

WHITHER away delight ?
Thou cam'st but now ; wilt thou so soon depart,
            And give me up to night ?
For many weeks of lingring pain and smart
But one half houre of comfort for my heart ?

            Me thinks delight should have
More skill in musick, and keep better time.
            Wert thou a winde or wave,
They quickly go and come with lesser crime :
Flowers look about, and die not in their prime.

            Thy short abode and stay
Feeds not, but addes to the desire of meat.
            Lime begg'd of old (they say)
A neighbour spring to cool his inward heat ;
Which by the springs accesse grew much more great.

            In hope of thee my heart
Pickt here and there a crumme, and would not die ;
            But constant to his part
When as my fears foretold this, did replie,
A slender thread a gentle guest will tie.

            Yet if the heart that wept
Must let thee go, return when it doth knock.
            Although thy heap be kept
For future times, the droppings of the stock
May oft break forth, and never break the lock.

            If I have more to spinne,
The wheel shall go, so that thy stay be short.

Thou knowst how grief and sinne
Disturb the work.　O make me not their sport,
Who by thy coming may be made a court !

THE PULLEY ✕

WHEN God at first made man,
Having a glasse of blessings standing by ;
Let us (said he) poure on him all we can :
Let the worlds riches, which dispersed lie,
　　　Contract into a span.

So strength first made a way ;
Then beautie flow'd, then wisdome, honour, pleasure :
When almost all was out, God made a stay,
Perceiving that alone of all his treasure
　　　Rest in the bottome lay.

For if I should (said he)
Bestow this jewell also on my creature,
He would adore my gifts instead of me,
And rest in Nature, not the God of Nature.
　　　So both should losers be.

Yet let him keep the rest,
But keep them with repining restlessnesse :
Let him be rich and wearie, that at least,
If goodnesse leade him not, yet wearinesse
　　　May tosse him to my breast.

THE FLOWER

How fresh, O Lord, how sweet and clean
Are thy returns ! ev'n as the flowers in spring ;
　　　To which, besides their own demean,
The late-past frosts tributes of pleasure bring.

Grief melts away
Like snow in May,
As if there were no such cold thing.

Who would have thought my shrivel'd heart
Could have recover'd greennesse ?   It was gone
Quite under ground ; as flowers depart
To see their mother-root, when they have blown ;
Where they together
All the hard weather,
Dead to the world, keep house unknown.

These are thy wonders, Lord of power,
Killing and quickning, bringing down to hell
And up to heaven in an houre ;
Making a chiming of a passing-bell.
We say amisse,
This or that is :
Thy word is all, if we could spell.

O that I once past changing were,
Fast in thy Paradise, where no flower can wither :
Many a spring I shoot up fair,
Offring at heav'n, growing and groning thither :
Nor doth my flower
Want a spring-showre,
My sinnes and I joining together :

But while I grow in a straight line,
Still upwards bent, as if heav'n were mine own,
Thy anger comes, and I decline :
What frost to that ? what pole is not the zone,
Where all things burn,
When thou dost turn,
And the least frown of thine is shown ?

And now in age I bud again,
After so many deaths I live and write ;

I once more smell the dew and rain,
And relish versing : O my onely light,
   It cannot be
   That I am he
On whom thy tempests fell all night.

These are thy wonders, Lord of love,
To make us see we are but flowers that glide :
  Which when we once can finde and prove,
Thou hast a garden for us, where to bide.
   Who would be more,
   Swelling through store,
Forfeit their Paradise by their pride.

DOTAGE

FALSE glozing pleasures, casks of happinesse,
Foolish night-fires, womens and childrens wishes,
Chases in Arras, guilded emptinesse,
Shadows well mounted, dreams in a career,
Embroider'd lyes, nothing between two dishes ;
   These are the pleasures here.

True earnest sorrows, rooted miseries,
Anguish in grain, vexations ripe and blown,
Sure-footed griefs, solid calamities,
Plain demonstrations, evident and cleare,
Fetching their proofs ev'n from the very bone ;
   These are the sorrows here.

But oh the folly of distracted men,
Who griefs in earnest, joyes in jest pursue ;
Preferring, like brute beasts, a lothsome den
Before a court, ev'n that above so cleare,
Where are no sorrows, but delights more true,
   Then miseries are here !

THE SONNE

LET forrain nations of their language boast,
What fine varietie each tongue affords :
I like our language, as our men and coast :
Who cannot dresse it well, want wit, not words.
How neatly doe we give one onely name
To parents issue and the sunnes bright starre !
A sonne is light and fruit ; a fruitfull flame
Chasing the fathers dimnesse, carri'd farre
From the first man in th' East, to fresh and new
Western discov'ries of posteritie.
So in one word our Lords humilitie
We turn upon him in a sense most true :
    For what Christ once in humblenesse began
    We him in glorie call, *The Sonne of Man.*

A TRUE HYMNE

    MY joy, my life, my crown !
  My heart was meaning all the day,
    Somewhat it fain would say :
And still it runneth mutt'ring up and down
With onely this, *My joy, my life, my crown.*

    Yet slight not these few words :
  If truly said, they may take part
    Among the best in art.
The finenesse which a hymne or psalme affords,
Is, when the soul unto the lines accords.

    He who craves all the minde,
  And all the soul, and strength, and time,
    If the words onely ryme,
Justly complains, that somewhat is behinde
To make his verse, or write a hymne in kinde.

Whereas if th' heart be moved,
Although the verse be somewhat scant,
God doth supplie the want.
As when th' heart sayes (sighing to be approved)
O, could I love ! and stops : God writeth, *Loved.*

THE ANSWER

My comforts drop and melt away like snow :
I shake my head, and all the thoughts and ends,
Which my fierce youth did bandie, fall and flow
Like leaves about me ; or like summer friends,
Flyes of estates and sunne-shine.   But to all,
Who think me eager, hot, and undertaking,
But in my prosecutions slack and small ;
As a young exhalation, newly waking,
Scorns his first bed of dirt, and means the sky ;
But cooling by the way, grows pursie and slow,
And setling to a cloud, doth live and die
In that dark state of tears : to all, that so
     Show me, and set me, I have one reply,
Which they that know the rest, know more then I.

THE ROSE

Presse me not to take more pleasure
     In this world of sugred lies,
And to use a larger measure
     Then my strict, yet welcome size.

First, there is no pleasure here :
     Colour'd griefs indeed there are,
Blushing woes, that look as cleare
     As if they could beautie spare.

Or if such deceits there be,
  Such delights I meant to say ;
There are no such things to me,
  Who have pass'd my right away.

But I will not much oppose
  Unto what you now advise :
Onely take this gentle rose,
  And therein my answer lies.

What is fairer then a rose ?
  What is sweeter ? yet it purgeth
Purgings enmitie disclose,
  Enmitie forbearance urgeth.

If then all that worldlings prize
  Be contracted to a rose ;
Sweetly there indeed it lies,
  But it biteth in the close.

So this flower doth judge and sentence
  Worldly joyes to be a scourge :
For they all produce repentance,
  And repentance is a purge.

But I health, not physick choose :
  Onely though I you oppose,
Say that fairly I refuse,
  For my answer is a rose.

THE ELIXER

Teach me, my God and King,
  In all things thee to see,
And what I do in any thing,
  To do it as for thee :

Not rudely, as a beast,
To runne into an action ;
But still to make thee prepossest,
And give it his perfection.

A man that looks on glasse,
On it may stay his eye ;
Or if he pleaseth, through it passe,
And then the heav'n espie.

All may of thee partake :
Nothing can be so mean,
Which with his tincture (for thy sake)
Will not grow bright and clean.

A servant with this clause
Makes drudgerie divine :
Who sweeps a room, as for thy laws,
Makes that and th' action fine.

This is the famous stone
That turneth all to gold :
For that which God doth touch and own
Cannot for lesse be told.

DOOMS-DAY

COME away,
Make no delay.
Summon all the dust to rise,
Till it stirre, and rubbe the eyes ;
While this member jogs the other,
Each one whispring, *Live you brother ?*

Come away,
Make this the day.

Dust, alas, no musick feels,
But thy trumpet : then it kneels,
As peculiar notes and strains
Cure Tarantulaes raging pains.

     Come away,
    O make no stay !
Let the graves make their confession,
Lest at length they plead possession :
Fleshes stubbornnesse may have
Read that lesson to the grave.

     Come away,
    Thy flock doth stray.
Some to windes their bodie lend,
And in them may drown a friend :
Some in noisome vapours grow
To a plague and publick wo.

     Come away,
    Help our decay.
Man is out of order hurl'd,
Parcel'd out to all the world.
Lord, thy broken consort raise,
And the musick shall be praise.

RICHARD CRASHAW

RICHARD CRASHAW

SAINT MARY MAGDALENE, OR, THE WEEPER

Lo! where a wounded heart with bleeding eyes conspire,
Is she a flaming fountain or a weeping fire?

THE WEEPER

I

HAIL, sister springs!
Parents of silver-footed rills!
Ever-bubbling things!
Thawing crystal! snowy hills
Still spending, never spent! I mean
Thy fair eyes, sweet Magdalene!

II

Heavens thy fair eyes be;
Heavens of ever-falling stars.
'Tis seed-time still with thee;
And stars thou sow'st, whose harvest dares
Promise the Earth to countershine
Whatever makes Heaven's forehead fine.

III

But we are deceivèd all:
Stars indeed they are too true:
For they but seem to fall,
As Heaven's other spangles do;
It is not for our Earth and us,
To shine in things so precious.

IV

    Upwards thou dost weep,
  Heaven's bosom drinks the gentle stream.
    Where th' milky rivers creep,
  Thine floats above, and is the cream.
Waters above th' heavens, what they be
We are taught best by thy tears and thee.

V

    Every morn from hence,
  A brisk cherub something sips,
    Whose sacred influence
  Adds sweetness to his sweetest lips ;
Then to his music ; and his song
Tastes of this breakfast all day long.

VI

    When some new bright guest
  Takes up among the stars a room,
    And Heaven will make a feast :
  Angels with crystal phials come
And draw from these full eyes of thine,
Their Master's water, their own wine.

VII

    The dew no more will weep
  The primrose's pale cheek to deck :
    The dew no more will sleep
  Nuzzel'd in the lily's neck ;
Much rather would it be thy tear,
And leave them both to tremble here.

VIII

Not the soft gold which
Steals from the amber-weeping tree,
Makes Sorrow half so rich
As the drops distill'd from thee.
Sorrow's best jewels lie in these
Caskets, of which Heaven keeps the keys.

IX

When Sorrow would be seen
In her brightest majesty :
(For she is a Queen) :
Then is she dress'd by none but thee.
Then, and only then, she wears
Her proudest pearls : I mean, thy tears.

X

Not in the Evening's eyes,
When they red with weeping are
For the Sun that dies,
Sits Sorrow with a face so fair.
Nowhere but here did ever meet
Sweetness so sad, sadness so sweet.

XI

Sadness all the while
She sits in such a throne as this,
Can do nought but smile,
Nor believes she Sadness is :
Gladness itself would be more glad,
To be made so sweetly sad.

XII

There's no need at all,
That the balsam-sweating bough

So coyly should let fall
    His med'cinable tears ; for now
Nature has learnt to extract a dew
More sovereign and sweet, from you.

XIII

    Yet let the poor drops weep,
    (Weeping is the ease of Woe) :
    Softly let them creep,
    Sad that they are vanquish'd so.
They, though to others no relief,
Balsam may be for their own grief.

XIV

    Golden though he be,
    Golden Tagus murmurs through ;
    Were his way by thee,
    Content and quiet he would go ;
So much more rich would he esteem
Thy silver, than his golden stream.

XV

    Well does the May that lies
    Smiling in thy cheeks, confess
    The April in thine eyes ;
    Mutual sweetness they express.
No April e'er lent kinder showers,
Nor May returned more faithful flowers.

XVI

    O cheeks !   Beds of chaste loves,
    By your own showers seasonably dashed.
    Eyes !   Nests of milky doves,
    In your own wells decently washed.
O wit of Love ! that thus could place
Fountain and garden in one face.

XVII

O sweet contest of woes
With loves ; of tears with smiles disputing !
O fair and friendly foes,
Each other kissing and confuting !
While rain and sunshine, cheeks and eyes,
Close in kind contrarieties.

XVIII

But can these fair floods be
Friends with the bosom-fires that fill thee ?
Can so great flames agree
Eternal tears should thus distil thee ?
O floods ! O fires ! O suns ! O showers !
Mixed and made friends by Love's sweet powers.

XIX

'Twas His well-pointed dart
That digged these wells, and dressed this wine ;
And taught the wounded heart
The way into these weeping eyne.
Vain loves avaunt ! bold hands forbear !
The Lamb hath dipped His white foot here.

XX

And now where'er He stays,
Among the Galilean mountains,
Or more unwelcome ways ;
He's followed by two faithful fountains ;
Two walking baths, two weeping motions,
Portable, and compendious oceans.

XXI

O thou, thy Lord's fair store !
In thy so rich and rare expenses,

Even when He showed most poor
He might provoke the wealth of Princes.
What Prince's wanton'st pride e'er could
Wash with silver, wipe with gold?

XXII

Who is that King, but He
Who calls't His crown, to be called thine,
That thus can boast to be
Waited on by a wandering mine,
A voluntary mint, that strowes
Warm silver showers where'er He goes?

XXIII

O precious prodigal!
Fair spendthrift of thyself! thy measure
(Merciless love!) is all.
Even to the last pearl in thy treasure:
All places, times, and objects be
Thy tears' sweet opportunity.

XXIV

Does the day-star rise?
Still thy tears do fall and fall.
Does Day close his eyes?
Still the fountain weeps for all.
Let Night or Day do what they will,
Thou hast thy task: thou weepest still.

XXV

Does thy song lull the air?
Thy falling tears keep faithful time.
Does thy sweet-breathed prayer
Up in clouds of incense climb?
Still at each sigh, that is each stop,
A bead, that is a tear, does drop.

XXVI

At these thy weeping gates
(Watching their watery motion),
Each wingèd moment waits :
Takes his tear, and gets him gone.
By thine eyes' tinct ennobled thus,
Time lays him up ; he's precious.

XXVII

Time, as by thee He passes,
Makes thy ever-watery eyes
His hour-glasses.
By them His steps He rectifies.
The sands He used no longer please,
For His own sands He'll use thy seas.

XXVIII

Not, " so long she livèd,"
Shall thy tomb report of thee ;
But, " so long she grievèd " :
Thus must we date thy memory.
Others by moments, months, and years
Measure their ages ; thou, by tears.

XXIX

So do perfumes expire,
So sigh tormented sweets, opprest
With proud unpitying fire,
Such tears the suffering rose, that's vext
With ungentle flames, does shed,
Sweating in a too warm bed.

XXX

Say, ye bright brothers,
The fugitive sons of those fair eyes,
Your fruitful mothers,
What make you here ? what hopes can 'tice
You to be born ? what cause can borrow
You from those nests of noble sorrow ?

XXXI

Whither away so fast ?
For sure the sluttish earth
Your sweetness cannot taste,
Nor does the dust deserve your birth.
Sweet, whither haste you then ?   O say
Why you trip so fast away ?

XXXII

We go not to seek
The darling of Aurora's bed,
The rose's modest cheek,
Nor the violet's humble head.
Though the field's eyes too Weepers be,
Because they want such tears as we.

XXXIII

Much less mean we to trace
The fortune of inferior gems,
Preferr'd to some proud face,
Or perched upon fear'd diadems :
Crown'd heads are toys.   We go to meet
A worthy object, our Lord's feet.

PSALM CXXXVII

ON the proud banks of great Euphrates' flood,
  There we sate, and there we wept :
Our harps, that now no music understood,
  Nodding, on the willows slept :
    While unhappy captived we,
    Lovely Sion, thought on thee.
They, they that snatch'd us from our country's breast
  Would have a song carved to their ears
In Hebrew numbers, then (O cruel jest)
  When harps and hearts were drown'd in tears :
    Come, they cried, come sing and play
    One of Sion's songs to-day.
Sing ? play ? to whom (ah !) shall we sing or play,
  If not, Jerusalem, to thee ?
Ah ! thee, Jerusalem, ah ! sooner may
  This hand forget the mastery
    Of Music's dainty touch, than I
    The music of thy memory.
Which, when I lose, O may at once my tongue
  Lose this same busy-speaking art ;
Unperched, her vocal arteries unstrung,
  No more acquainted with my heart,
    On my dry palate's roof to rest
    A withered leaf, an idle guest.
No, no, Thy good, Sion, alone must crown
  The head of all thy hope-nursed joys.
But Edom, cruel thou, thou criedst down, down
  Sink Sion, down and never rise ;
    Her falling thou didst urge and thrust,
    And haste to dash her into dust :
Dost laugh proud Babel's daughter ? do, laugh on,
  Till thy ruin teach thee tears,
Even such as these ; laugh, till a 'venging throng
  Of woes too late do rouse thy fears :
    Laugh till thy children's bleeding bones
    Weep precious tears upon the stones.

IN THE HOLY NATIVITY OF OUR LORD GOD

A HYMN SUNG AS BY THE SHEPHERDS

THE HYMN

Chorus

COME, ye shepherds, whose blest sight
Hath met Love's noon in Nature's night ;
    Come, lift we up our loftier song,
    And wake the sun that lies too long.

To all our world of well-stolen joy
He slept, and dreamt of no such thing.
    While we found out Heaven's fairer eye,
And kissed the cradle of our King.
    Tell Him he rises now, too late
To show us aught worth looking at.

Tell him we now can show him more
Than he e'er show'd to mortal sight ;
    Than he himself e'er saw before,
Which to be seen needs not his light.
    Tell him, Tityrus, where th' hast been,
Tell him, Thyrsis, what th' hast seen.

Tityrus

Gloomy night embraced the place
Where the noble Infant lay.
    The Babe looked up and showed His face ;
In spite of darkness, it was day.
    It was Thy day, Sweet, and did rise,
Not from the East, but from Thine eyes.

Chorus

It was Thy day, Sweet . . .

Thyrsis

Winter chid aloud, and sent
The angry North to wage his wars.
  The North forgot his fierce intent,
And left perfumes instead of scars.
  By those sweet eyes' persuasive powers,
Where he meant frost, he scattered flowers.

Chorus

By those sweet eyes' . . .

Both

We saw Thee in Thy balmy nest,
Young dawn of our eternal Day ;
  We saw Thine eyes break from their East,
And chase the trembling shades away.
  We saw Thee, and we blest the sight,
We saw Thee by Thine Own sweet light.

Tityrus

Poor world (said I), what wilt thou do
To entertain this starry Stranger ?
  Is this the best thou canst bestow,
A cold, and not too cleanly, manger ?
  Contend, the powers of Heaven and Earth,
To fit a bed for this huge birth ?

Chorus

Contend, the powers . . .

Thyrsis

Proud world, said I, cease your contest,
And let the mighty Babe alone.
  The phœnix builds the phœnix' nest,
Love's architecture is his own.
  The Babe whose birth embraves this morn,
Made His Own bed ere He was born.

Chorus

The Babe whose . . .

Tityrus

I saw the curled drops, soft and slow,
Come hovering o'er the place's head ;
  Offering their whitest sheets of snow
To furnish the fair Infant's bed :
  Forbear, said I ; be not too bold,
Your fleece is white, but 'tis too cold.

Chorus

Forbear, said I . . . .

Thyrsis

I saw the obsequious Seraphim
Their rosy fleece of fire bestow,
  For well they now can spare their wing,
Since Heaven itself lies here below.
  Well done, said I, but are you sure
Your down so warm, will pass for pure ?

Chorus

Well done, said I . . .

Tityrus

No, no, your King's not yet to seek
Where to repose His royal head ;
  See, see, how soon His new-bloom'd cheek
'Twixt's Mother's breasts is gone to bed.
  Sweet choice, said we, no way but so
Not to lie cold, yet sleep in snow.

Chorus

Sweet choice, said we . . .

Both

We saw Thee in Thy balmy nest,
Bright dawn of our eternal Day !
  We saw Thine eyes break from their East,
And chase the trembling shades away.
  We saw Thee, and we blest the sight,
We saw Thee by Thine Own sweet light.

Chorus

We saw Thee . . .

Full Chorus

Welcome, all wonders in one sight,
Eternity shut in a span,
  Summer in Winter, Day in Night,
Heaven in Earth, and God in man,
  Great, little One, whose all-embracing birth
Lifts Earth to Heaven, stoops Heaven to Earth.
  Welcome, though not to gold nor silk,
To more than Cæsar's birthright is,
  Two sister-seas of virgin-milk,
With many a rarely-tempered kiss,

That breathes at once both maid and mother,
Warms in the one, cools in the other.
   She sings Thy tears asleep, and dips
Her kisses in Thy weeping eye ;
   She spreads the red leaves of Thy lips,
That in their buds yet blushing lie :
   She 'gainst those mother-diamonds, tries
The points of Her young eagle's eyes.

   Welcome, though not to those gay flies,
Gilded i' th' beams of earthly kings,
   Slippery souls in smiling eyes ;
But to poor shepherds' home-spun things ;
   Whose wealth's their flock ; whose wit, to be
Well-read in their simplicity.

   Yet when young April's husband-showers
Shall bless the fruitful Maia's bed,
   We'll bring the first-born of her flowers
To kiss Thy feet, and crown Thy head.
   To Thee, dread Lamb, Whose love must keep
The shepherds, more than they the sheep.

   To Thee, meek Majesty, soft King
Of simple Graces and sweet Loves :
   Each of us his lamb will bring,
Each his pair of silver doves ;
   Till burnt at last in fire of Thy fair eyes,
Ourselves become our own best sacrifice.

PRAYER

AN ODE WHICH WAS PREFIXED TO A LITTLE PRAYER-
BOOK GIVEN TO A YOUNG GENTLEWOMAN

Lo here a little volume, but great book !
    (Fear it not, sweet,
      It is no hypocrite),
Much larger in itself than in its look.

A nest of new-born sweets ;
Whose native fires disdaining
To lie thus folded, and complaining
Of these ignoble sheets,
Affect more comely bands
(Fair one) from thy kind hands ;
And confidently look
To find the rest
Of a rich binding in your breast.
It is, in one choice handful, Heaven and all
Heaven's royal host ; encamp'd thus small
To prove that true, Schools use to tell,
Ten thousand angels in one point can dwell.
It is Love's great artillery
Which here contracts itself, and comes to lie
Close-couch'd in your white bosom ; and from thence,
As from a snowy fortress of defence,
Against the ghostly foes to take your part,
And fortify the hold of your chaste heart.
It is an armoury of light ;
Let constant use but keep it bright,
    You'll find it yields,
To holy hands and humble hearts,
    More swords and shields
Than sin hath snares, or Hell hath darts.
    Only be sure
    The hands be pure
That hold these weapons ; and the eyes
    Those of turtles, chaste and true ;
Wakeful and wise :
    Here is a friend shall fight for you,
Hold but this book before your heart,
Let Prayer alone to play his part ;
But O the heart,
That studies this high art,
Must be a sure house-keeper :
And yet no sleeper.
Dear soul, be strong,

Mercy will come ere long,
And bring his bosom fraught with blessings,
Flowers of never-fading graces,
To make immortal dressings
For worthy souls, whose wise embraces
Store up themselves for Him, Who is alone
The Spouse of virgins, and the Virgin's Son.
But if the noble Bridegroom, when He come,
    Shall find the loitering heart from home ;
    Leaving her chaste abode
    To gad abroad
Among the gay mates of the god of flies ;
    To take her pleasure, and to play
    And keep the devil's holiday ;
To dance in th' sunshine of some smiling
    But beguiling
Sphere of sweet and sugar'd lies ;
    Some slippery pair,
    Of false, perhaps as fair,
Flattering but forswearing, eyes ;
Doubtless some other heart
    Will get the start
Meanwhile, and stepping in before,
Will take possession of the sacred store
Of hidden sweets and holy joys ;
Words which are not heard with ears
(Those tumultuous shops of noise)
Effectual whispers, whose still voice
The soul itself more feels than hears ;
Amorous languishments, luminous trances ;
Sights which are not seen with eyes ;
Spiritual and soul-piercing glances,
Whose pure and subtle lightning flies
Home to the heart, and sets the house on fire
And melts it down in sweet desire :
    Yet does not stay
To ask the windows' leave to pass that way ;
Delicious deaths, soft exhalations ;

A thousand unknown rites
 Of joys, and rarefied delights ;
An hundred thousand goods, glories, and graces ;
 And many a mystic thing,
 Which the divine embraces
Of the dear Spouse of spirits, with them will bring ;
 For which it is no shame
That dull mortality must not know a name.
Of all this hidden store
Of blessings, and ten thousand more
 (If when He come
 He find the heart from home)
 Doubtless He will unload
 Himself some otherwhere,
 And pour abroad
 His precious sweets
On the fair soul whom first He meets.
O fair ! O fortunate ! O rich ! O dear !
 O happy and thrice-happy she,
 Dear silver-breasted dove
 Whoe'er she be,
 Whose early love
 With wingèd vows,
Makes haste to meet her morning Spouse,
And close with His immortal kisses.
 Happy indeed who never misses
 To improve that precious hour,
 And every day
 Seize her sweet prey,
All fresh and fragrant as He rises,
Dropping with a balmy shower
A delicious dew of spices ;
O let the blissful heart hold fast
Her heavenly armful ; she shall taste
At once ten thousand paradises ;
 She shall have power
 To rifle and deflower
The rich and roseal spring of those rare sweets,

Which with a swelling bosom there she meets :
Boundless and infinite, bottomless treasures
Of pure inebriating pleasures.
Happy proof ! she shall discover
    What joy, what bliss,
    How many heavens at once it is
To have her God become her Lover.

TO THE SAME

COUNSEL CONCERNING HER CHOICE

DEAR, Heaven designèd soul,
    Amongst the rest
Of suitors that besiege your maiden breast
    Why may not I
    My fortune try
And venture to speak one good word,
Not for myself, alas ! but for my dearer Lord ?
You have seen already in this lower sphere
Of froth and bubbles, what to look for here :
Say, gentle soul, what can you find
    But painted shapes,
    Peacocks and apes,
    Illustrious flies,
Gilded dunghills, glorious lies ;
    Goodly surmises
    And deep disguises,
Oaths of water, words of wind ?
Truth bids me say 'tis time you cease to trust
Your soul to any son of dust.
'Tis time you listen to a braver love,
    Which from above
    Calls you up higher
    And bids you come
    And choose your room
Among His own fair sons of fire ·

Where you among
The golden throng,
That watches at His palace doors,
May pass along,
And follow those fair stars of yours ;
Stars much too fair and pure to wait upon
The false smiles of a sublunary sun.
Sweet, let me prophesy that at last 't will prove
Your wary love
Lays up his purer and more precious vows,
And means them for a far more worthy Spouse
Than this World of lies can give ye :
Even for Him, with Whom nor cost,
Nor love, nor labour can be lost ;
Him Who never will deceive ye.
Let not my Lord, the mighty Lover
Of souls, disdain that I discover
The hidden art
Of His high stratagem to win your heart :
It was His heavenly art
Kindly to cross you
In your mistaken love ;
That, at the next remove
Thence, He might toss you
And strike your troubled heart
Home to Himself, to hide it in His breast,
The bright ambrosial nest
Of love, of life, and everlasting rest.
Happy mistake !
That thus shall wake
Your wise soul, never to be won
Now with a love below the sun.
Your first choice fails ; O when you choose again
May it not be among the sons of men !

DESCRIPTION OF A RELIGIOUS HOUSE AND CONDITION OF LIFE

(OUT OF BARCLAY)

No roofs of gold o'er riotous tables shining,
Whole days and suns devour'd with endless dining.
No sails of Tyrian silk, proud pavements sweeping,
Nor ivory couches costlier slumber keeping ;
False lights of flaring gems ; tumultuous joys ;
Halls full of flattering men and frisking boys ;
Whate'er false shows of short and slippery good
Mix the mad sons of men in mutual blood.
But walks and unshorn woods ; and souls, just so
Unforced and genuine ; but not shady though.
Our lodgings hard and homely as our fare,
That chaste and cheap, as the few clothes we wear ;
Those, coarse and negligent, as the natural locks
Of these loose groves ; rough as th' unpolish'd rocks.
A hasty portion of prescribèd sleep ;
Obedient slumbers, that can wake and weep,
And sing, and sigh, and work, and sleep again ;
Still rolling a round sphere of still-returning pain.
Hands full of hearty labours ; pains that pay
And prize themselves ; do much, that more they may,
And work for work, not wages ; let to-morrow's
New drops, wash off the sweat of this day's sorrows.
A long and daily-dying life, which breathes
A respiration of reviving deaths.
But neither are there those ignoble stings
That nip the blossom of the World's best things,
And lash Earth-labouring souls. . . .
No cruel guard of diligent cares, that keep
Crown'd woes awake, as things too wise for sleep :
But reverent discipline, and religious fear,
And soft obedience, find sweet biding here ;

Silence, and sacred rest ; peace, and pure joys ;
Kind loves keep house, lie close, and make no noise ;
And room enough for monarchs, while none swells.
Beyond the kingdoms of contentful cells.
The self-rememb'ring soul sweetly recovers
Her kindred with the stars ; not basely hovers
Below : but meditates her immortal way
Home to the original source of Light and intellectual day.

ON MR. GEORGE HERBERT'S BOOK, ENTITLED,
THE TEMPLE OF SACRED POEMS

SENT TO A GENTLEWOMAN

KNOW you, fair, on what you look ?
Divinest love lies in this book :
Expecting fire from your fair eyes,
To kindle this his sacrifice.
When your hands untie these strings,
Think you've an angel by the wings ;
One that gladly will be nigh,
To wait upon each morning sigh ;
To flutter in the balmy air,
Of your well-perfumèd prayer.
These white plumes of his he'll lend you,
Which every day to Heaven will send you :
To take acquaintance of the sphere,
And all the smooth-faced kindred there.
　　And though Herbert's name do owe
　　These devotions ; fairest, know
　　While I thus lay them on the shrine
　　Of your white hand, they are mine.

A HYMN, TO THE NAME AND HONOUR OF THE ADMIRABLE SAINT TERESA:

Foundress of the Reformation of the discalced Carmelites, both men and women; a woman for angelical height of speculation, for masculine courage of performance more than a woman; who yet a child outran maturity, and durst plot a martyrdom.

Misericordias Domini in Æternum Cantabo.

THE HYMN

Love, thou art absolute sole lord
Of life and death.   To prove the word
We'll now appeal to none of all
Those thy old soldiers, great and tall,
Ripe men of martyrdom, that could reach down,
With strong arms, their triumphant crown ;
Such as could with lusty breath,
Speak loud into the face of Death
Their great Lord's glorious Name, to none
Of those whose spacious bosoms spread a throne
For Love at large to fill ; spare blood and sweat :
And see him take a private seat,
Making his mansion in the mild
And milky soul of a soft child.
    Scarce has she learnt to lisp the name
Of martyr ; yet she thinks it shame
Life should so long play with that breath
Which spent can buy so brave a death.
She never undertook to know
What Death with Love should have to do ;
Nor has she e'er yet understood
Why to show love, she should shed blood,
Yet though she cannot tell you why,
She can love, and she can die.
    Scarce has she blood enough to make
A guilty sword blush for her sake ;

Yet has she a heart dares hope to prove
How much less strong is Death than Love.
   Be Love but there, let poor six years
Be posed with the maturest fears
Man trembles at, you straight shall find
Love knows no nonage, nor the mind ;
'Tis love, not years or limbs that can
Make the martyr, or the man.
Love touched her heart, and lo it beats
High, and burns with such brave heats ;
Such thirsts to die, as dares drink up
A thousand cold deaths in one cup.
Good reason ; for she breathes all fire ;
Her white breast heaves with strong desire
Of what she may, with fruitless wishes,
Seek for amongst her mother's kisses.
   Since 'tis not to be had at home
She'll travel to a martyrdom.
No home for hers confesses she
But where she may a martyr be.
   She'll to the Moors ; and trade with them
For this unvalued diadem :
She'll offer them her dearest breath,
With Christ's name in't, in change for death :
She'll bargain with them, and will give
Them God, teach them how to live
In Him ; or, if they this deny,
For Him she'll teach them how to die.
So shall she leave amongst them sown
Her Lord's blood, or at least her own.
   Farewell then, all the World adieu ;
Teresa is no more for you.
Farewell, all pleasures, sports, and joys
(Never till now esteemèd toys).
Farewell, whatever dear may be,
Mother's arms, or father's knee :
Farewell house, and farewell home !
She's for the Moors, and martyrdom.

5

Sweet, not so fast ! lo, thy fair Spouse
Whom thou seek'st with so swift vows ;
Calls thee back, and bids thee come
T' embrace a milder martyrdom.
　　Blest powers forbid, thy tender life
Should bleed upon a barbarous knife :
Or some base hand have power to rase
Thy breast's chaste cabinet, and uncase
A soul kept there so sweet : O no,
Wise Heaven will never have it so.
Thou art Love's victim ; and must die
A death more mystical and high :
Into Love's arms thou shalt let fall
A still-surviving funeral.
His is the dart must make the death
Whose stroke shall taste thy hallowed breath ;
A dart thrice dipp'd in that rich flame
Which writes thy Spouse's radiant Name
Upon the roof of Heaven, where aye
It shines ; and with a sovereign ray
Beats bright upon the burning faces
Of souls which in that Name's sweet graces
Find everlasting smiles : so rare,
So spiritual, pure, and fair
Must be th' immortal instrument
Upon whose choice point shall be sent
A life so loved : and that there be
Fit executioners for thee,
The fairest and first-born sons of fire.
Blest seraphim, shall leave their quire,
And turn Love's soldiers, upon thee
To exercise their archery.
　　O how oft shalt thou complain
Of a sweet and subtle pain :
Of intolerable joys :
Of a death, in which who dies
Loves his death, and dies again,
And would for ever so be slain.

And lives, and dies ; and knows not why
To live, but that he thus may never leave to die.
    How kindly will thy gentle heart
Kiss the sweetly-killing dart,
And close in his embraces keep
Those delicious wounds, that weep
Balsam to heal themselves with ; thus
When these thy deaths, so numerous,
Shall all at last die into one,
And melt thy soul's sweet mansion ;
Like a soft lump of incense, hasted
By too hot a fire, and wasted
Into perfuming clouds, so fast
Shalt thou exhale to Heaven at last
In a resolving sigh, and then
O what ?   Ask not the tongues of men ;
Angels cannot tell ; suffice
Thyself shalt feel thine own full joys,
And hold them fast for ever there.
So soon as thou shalt first appear,
The moon of maiden stars, thy white
Mistress, attended by such bright
Souls as thy shining self, shall come
And in her first ranks make thee room ;
Where 'mongst her snowy family
Immortal welcomes wait for thee.
    O what delight, when revealed Life shall stand,
And teach thy lips Heaven with His hand ;
On which thou now may'st to thy wishes
Heap up thy consecrated kisses.
What joys shall seize thy soul, when She,
Bending her blessed eyes on Thee,
(Those second smiles of Heaven,) shall dart
Her mild rays through Thy melting heart.
    Angels, thy old friends, there shall greet thee,
Glad at their own home now to meet thee.
    All thy good works which went before
And waited for thee, at the door,

Shall own thee there ; and all in one
Weave a constellation
Of crowns, with which the King thy Spouse
Shall build up thy triumphant brows.

All thy old woes shall now smile on thee,
And thy pains sit bright upon thee,
All thy sorrows here shall shine,
All thy sufferings be divine :
Tears shall take comfort, and turn gems,
And wrongs repent to diadems.
Even thy death shall live ; and new
Dress the soul, that erst he slew.
Thy wounds shall blush to such bright scars
As keep account of the Lamb's wars.

Those rare works where thou shalt leave writ
Love's noble history, with wit
Taught thee by none but Him, while here
They feed our souls, shall clothe thine there.
Each heavenly word, by whose hid flame
Our hard hearts shall strike fire, the same
Shall flourish on thy brows, and be
Both fire to us and flame to thee ;
Whose light shall live bright in thy face
By glory, in our hearts by grace.

Thou shalt look round about, and see
Thousands of crown'd souls throng to be
Themselves thy crown : sons of thy vows,
The virgin-births with which thy sovereign Spouse
Made fruitful thy fair soul.   Go now
And with them all about thee, bow
To Him ; put on, (He'll say,) put on
(My rosy love) that thy rich zone
Sparkling with the sacred flames
Of thousand souls, whose happy names
Heaven keep upon thy score : (Thy bright
Life brought them first to kiss the light,
That kindled them to stars,) and so
Thou with the Lamb, thy Lord, shalt go,

And wheresoe'er He sets His white
Steps, walk with Him those ways of light,
Which who in death would live to see,
Must learn in life to die like thee.

AN APOLOGY FOR THE FOREGOING HYMN

AS HAVING BEEN WRIT WHEN THE AUTHOR WAS YET AMONG THE PROTESTANTS

THUS have I back again to thy bright name,
(Fair flood of holy fires !) transfus'd the flame
I took from reading thee ; 'tis to thy wrong,
I know, that in my weak and worthless song
Thou here art set to shine, where thy full day
Scarce dawns.   O pardon, if I dare to say
Thine own dear books are guilty.   For from thence
I learn'd to know that Love is eloquence.
That hopeful maxim gave me heart to try
If, what to other tongues is tuned so high,
Thy praise might not speak English too : forbid
(By all thy mysteries that there lie hid)
Forbid it, mighty Love ! let no fond hate
Of names and words so far prejudicate.
Souls are not Spaniards too : one friendly flood
Of Baptism blends them all into a blood.
Christ's Faith makes but one body of all souls,
And Love's that body's soul ; no law controls
Our free traffic for Heaven ; we may maintain
Peace, sure, with piety, though it come from Spain,
What soul soe'er in any language, can
Speak Heav'n like hers, is my soul's countryman.
O 'tis not Spanish, but 'tis Heav'n she speaks,
'Tis Heav'n that lies in ambush there, and breaks
From thence into the wondering reader's breast ;
Who feels his warm heart hatch into a nest
Of little eagles and young loves, whose high

Flights scorn the lazy dust, and things that die.
There are enow whose draughts (as deep as Hell)
Drink up all Spain in sack.   Let my soul swell
With the strong wine of Love : let others swim
In puddles ; we will pledge these Seraphim
Bowls full of richer blood than blush of grape
Was ever guilty of.   Change we our shape,
(My soul) some drink from men to beasts, O then
Drink we till we prove more, not less than men,
And turn not beasts, but angels.   Let the King
Me ever into these His cellars bring,
Where flows such wine as we can have of none
But Him Who trod the wine-press all alone :
Wine of youth. life, and the sweet deaths of Love ;
Wine of immortal mixture ; which can prove
Its tincture from the rosy nectar ; wine
That can exalt weak earth ; and so refine
Our dust, that, at one draught, Mortality
May drink itself up, and forget to die.

THE FLAMING HEART

UPON THE BOOK AND PICTURE OF THE SERAPHICAL SAINT TERESA AS SHE IS USUALLY EXPRESSED WITH A SERAPHIM BESIDE HER

WELL-MEANING readers, you that come as friends,
And catch the precious name this piece pretends ;
Make not too much haste to admire
That fair-cheek'd fallacy of fire.
That is a seraphim, they say,
And this the great Teresia.
Readers, be ruled by me ; and make
Here a well-placed and wise mistake ;
You must transpose the picture quite,
And spell it wrong to read it right ;

Read him for her, and her for him,
And call the saint the seraphim.
   Painter, what didst thou understand
To put her dart into his hand ?
See, even the years and size of him
Shows this the mother-seraphim.
This is the mistress-flame ; and duteous he
Her happy fire-works, here, comes down to see.
O most poor-spirited of men !
Had thy cold pencil kiss'd her pen,
Thou couldst not so unkindly err
To show us this faint shade for her.
Why, man, this speaks pure mortal frame ;
And mocks with female frost Love's manly flame.
One would suspect thou mean'st to paint
Some weak, inferior, woman-saint.
But had thy pale-faced purple took
Fire from the burning cheeks of that bright book,
Thou wouldst on her have heap'd up all
That could be found seraphical ;
Whate'er this youth of fire wears fair,
Rosy fingers, radiant hair,
Glowing cheek, and glist'ring wings,
All those fair and fragrant things,
But before all, that fiery dart
Had fill'd the hand of this great heart.
   Do then, as equal right requires ;
Since his the blushes be, and hers the fires,
Resume and rectify thy rude design ;
Undress thy seraphim into mine ;
Redeem this injury of thy art,
Give him the veil, give her the dart.
Give him the veil, that he may cover
The red cheeks of a rivall'd lover ;
Ashamed that our world now can show
Nests of new seraphim here below.
   Give her the dart, for it is she
(Fair youth) shoots both thy shaft and thee :

Say, all ye wise and well-pierced hearts
That live and die amidst her darts,
What is't your tasteful spirits do prove
In that rare life of her, and Love ?
Say, and bear witness.   Sends she not
A seraphim at every shot ?
What magazines of immortal arms there shine ꞉
Heaven's great artillery in each love-spun line.
Give then the dart to her who gives the flame ;
Give him the veil, who gives the shame.
    But if it be the frequent fate
Of worse faults to be fortunate ;
If all's prescription ; and proud wrong
Hearkens not to an humble song ;
For all the gallantry of him,
Give me the suffering seraphim.
His be the bravery of all those bright things,
The glowing cheeks, the glistering wings ;
The rosy hand, the radiant dart ;
Leave her alone the flaming heart.
    Leave her that ; and thou shalt leave her
Not one loose shaft, but Love's whole quiver ;
For in Love's field was never found
A nobler weapon than a wound.
Love's passives are his activ'st part :
The wounded is the wounding heart.
O heart ! the equal poise of Love's both parts,
Big alike with wound and darts,
Live in these conquering leaves ; live all the same ;
And walk through all tongues one triumphant flame.
Live here, great heart ; and love, and die, and kill ;
And bleed, and wound ; and yield and conquer still.
Let this immortal life where'er it comes
Walk in a crowd of loves and martyrdoms.
Let mystic deaths wait on't ; and wise souls be
The love-slain witnesses of this life of thee.
    O sweet incendiary ! show here thy art,
Upon this carcass of a hard cold heart ;

Let all thy scatter'd shafts of light that play
Among the leaves of thy large books of day,
Combined against this breast at once break in
And take away from me myself and sin ;
This gracious robbery shall thy bounty be,
And my best fortunes such fair spoils of me.
O thou undaunted daughter of desires !
By all thy dower of lights and fires ;
By all the eagle in thee, all the dove ;
By all thy lives and deaths of love ;
By thy large draughts of intellectual day,
And by thy thirsts of love more large than they ;
By all thy brim-fill'd bowls of fierce desire,
By thy last morning's draught of liquid fire ;
By the full kingdom of that final kiss
That seized thy parting soul, and seal'd thee His ;
By all the Heaven thou hast in Him
(Fair sister of the seraphim !)
By all of Him we have in thee ;
Leave nothing of myself in me.
Let me so read thy life, that I
Unto all life of mine may die.

A SONG OF DIVINE LOVE

LORD, when the sense of Thy sweet grace
Sends up my soul to seek Thy face,
Thy blessed eyes breed such desire,
I die in Love's delicious fire.

 O Love, I am thy sacrifice ;
Be still triumphant, blessed eyes ;
Still shine on me, fair suns, that I
Still may behold, though still I die.

Though still I die, I live again ;
Still longing so to be still slain ;

So gainful is such loss of breath ;
I die even in desire of death.
   Still live in me this loving strife
Of living death and dying life ;
For while Thou sweetly slayest me
Dead to myself, I live in Thee.

DIES IRÆ, DIES ILLA

THE HYMN OF THE CHURCH, IN MEDITATION OF THE DAY OF JUDGMENT

I

HEAR'ST thou, my soul, what serious things
Both the Psalm and Sibyl sings
Of a sure Judge, from Whose sharp ray
The World in flames shall fly away.

II

O that fire, before whose face
Heaven and Earth shall find no place.
O those eyes, Whose angry light
Must be the day of that dread night.

III

O that trump, whose blast shall run
An even round with the circling sun,
And urge the murmuring graves to bring
Pale mankind forth to meet his King.

IV

Horror of Nature, Hell, and Death,
When a deep groan from beneath
Shall cry, " We come, we come," and all
The caves of Night answer one call.

V

O that Book, whose leaves so bright
Will set the World in severe light.
O that Judge, Whose hand, Whose eye
None can endure ; yet none can fly.

VI

And then, poor soul, what wilt thou say ?
And to what patron choose to pray ?
When stars themselves shall stagger, and
The most firm foot no more then stand.

VII

But Thou givest leave (dread Lord !) that we
Take shelter from Thyself in Thee ;
And with the wings of Thine Own Dove
Fly to Thy sceptre of soft love.

VIII

Dear, remember in that Day
Who was the cause Thou cam'st this way.
Thy sheep was stray'd ; and Thou would'st be
Even lost Thyself in seeking me.

IX

Shall all that labour, all that cost
Of love, and even that loss, be lost ?
And this loved soul, judged worth no less
Than all that way and weariness ?

X

Just mercy, then, Thy reck'ning be
With my Price, and not with me ;
'Twas paid at first with too much pain,
To be paid twice, or once, in vain.

XI

Mercy (my Judge), mercy I cry
With blushing cheek and bleeding eye :
The conscious colours of my sin
Are red without and pale within.

XII

O let Thine Own soft bowels pay
Thyself, and so discharge that day.
If Sin can sigh, Love can forgive :
O say the word, my soul shall live !

XIII

Those mercies which Thy Mary found,
Or who Thy cross confess'd and crown'd,
Hope tells my heart, the same loves be
Still alive, and still for me.

XIV

Though both my prayers and tears combine,
Both worthless are ; for they are mine.
But Thou Thy bounteous Self still be ;
And show Thou art, by saving me.

XV

O when Thy last frown shall proclaim
The flocks of goats to folds of flame,
And all Thy lost sheep found shall be ;
Let, " Come, ye blessed," then call me.

XVI

When the dread " *Ite* " shall divide
Those limbs of death from Thy left side ;
Let those life-speaking lips command
That I inherit Thy right hand.

XVII

O hear a suppliant heart, all crushed
And crumbled into contrite dust.
My Hope, my Fear, my Judge, my Friend,
Take charge of me, and of my end.

CHARITAS NIMIA, OR, THE DEAR BARGAIN

LORD, what is man ? why should he cost Thee
So dear ? what had his ruin lost Thee ?
Lord, what is man, that Thou hast over-bought
So much a thing of nought ?

Love is too kind, I see ; and can
Make but a simple merchant-man.
'Twas for such sorry merchandise
Bold painters have put out his eyes.

Alas, sweet Lord, what were't to Thee
If there were no such worms as we ?
Heaven ne'ertheless still Heaven would be,
                Should mankind dwell
                In the deep Hell :
What have his woes to do with Thee ?

                Let him go weep
                O'er his own wounds ;
                Seraphim will not sleep,
Nor spheres let fall their faithful rounds.

                Still would the youthful spirits sing :
And still Thy spacious palace ring ;
Still would those beauteous ministers of light
                Burn all as bright,

And bow their flaming heads before Thee ;
Still thrones and dominations would adore Thee ;
Still would those ever-wakeful sons of fire
      Keep warm Thy praise
      Both nights and days,
And teach Thy loved name to their noble lyre.

Let froward dust then do its kind ;
And give itself for sport to the proud wind.
Why should a piece of peevish clay plead shares
In the eternity of Thy old cares ?
Why should'st Thou bow Thy awful breast to see
What mine own madnesses have done with me ?

Should not the king still keep his throne
Because some desperate fool's undone ?
Or will the World's illustrious eyes
Weep for every worm that dies ?

      Will the gallant sun
      E'er the less glorious run ?
Will he hang down his golden head,
Or e'er the sooner seek his Western bed,
      Because some foolish fly
      Grows wanton, and will die ?

If I were lost in misery,
What was it to Thy Heaven and Thee ?
What was it to Thy Precious Blood,
If my foul heart call'd for a flood ?
What if my faithless soul and I
      Would needs fall in
      With guilt and sin ;
What did the Lamb that He should die ?
What did the Lamb that He should need,
When the wolf sins, Himself to bleed ?

   If my base lust
Bargain'd with Death and well-beseeming dust :
   Why should the white
   Lamb's bosom write
   The purple name
   Of my sin's shame ?
Why should His unstain'd breast make good
My blushes with His Own heart-blood ?

O my Saviour, make me see
How dearly Thou hast paid for me ;
That lost again, my life may prove,
As then in death, so now in love.

ROBERT HERRICK

NOBLE NUMBERS

HIS CONFESSION

Look how our foule dayes do exceed our faire ;
And as our bad, more then our good works are,
Ev'n so those lines, pen'd by my wanton wit,
Treble the number of these good I've writ.
Things precious are least num'rous : men are prone
To do ten bad, for one good action.

HIS PRAYER FOR ABSOLUTION

For those my unbaptized rhimes,
Writ in my wild unhallowed times ;
For every sentence, clause, and word,
That's not inlaid with Thee, my Lord,
Forgive me, God, and blot each line
Out of my book, that is not Thine.
But if, 'mongst all, Thou find'st here one
Worthy Thy benediction ;
That one of all the rest, shall be
The glory of my work, and me.

TO FINDE GOD

Weigh me the fire ; or canst thou find
A way to measure out the wind ;
Distinguish all those floods that are
Mixt in that watrie theater ;

And tast thou them as saltlesse there,
As in their channell first they were.
Tell me the people that do keep
Within the kingdomes of the deep ;
Or fetch me back that cloud againe,
Beshiver'd into seeds of raine ;
Tell me the motes, dust, sands, and speares
Of corn, when Summer shakes his eares ;
Shew me that world of starres, and whence
They noiseless spill their influence :
This if thou canst ; then shew me Him
That rides the glorious cherubim.

WHAT GOD IS ✗

GOD is above the sphere of our esteem,
And is the best known, not defining Him.

UPON GOD

GOD is not onely said to be
An ens, but supraentitie.

MERCY AND LOVE

GOD hath two wings, which He doth ever move,
The one is mercy, and the next is love :
Under the first the sinners ever trust ;
And with the last He still directs the just.

GODS ANGER WITHOUT AFFECTION ✗

GOD when He's angry here with any one,
His wrath is free from perturbation ;
And when we think His looks are sowre and grim,
The alteration is in us, not Him.

GOD NOT TO BE COMPREHENDED

'TIS hard to finde God, but to comprehend
Him, as He is, is labour without end.

GODS PART

PRAYERS and praises are those spotlesse two
Lambs, by the law, which God requires as due.

AFFLICTION

GOD n'ere afflicts us more than our desert,
Though He may seem to over-act His part :
Sometimes He strikes us more than flesh can beare :
But yet still lesse then grace can suffer here.

THREE FATALL SISTERS

THREE fatall sisters wait upon each sin ;
First, Fear and Shame without, then Guilt within.

SILENCE

SUFFER thy legs, but not thy tongue to walk :
God, the most wise, is sparing of His talk.

MIRTH

TRUE mirth resides not in the smiling skin :
The sweetest solace is to act no sin.

LOADING AND UNLOADING

God loads, and unloads ; thus His work begins,
To load with blessings, and unload from sins.

GODS MERCY

Gods boundlesse mercy is, to sinfull man,
Like to the ever-wealthy ocean :
Which though it sends forth thousand streams, 'tis n'ere
Known, or els seen to be the emptier :
And though it takes all in, 'tis yet no more
Full, and fild-full, then when full-fild before.

PRAYERS MUST HAVE POISE

God He rejects all prayers that are sleight,
And want their poise : words ought to have their weight.

TO GOD

An Anthem, sung in the Chappell at White-Hall,
before the King

Verse.   My God, I'm wounded by my sin,
          And sore without, and sick within :
Ver. Chor. I come to Thee, in hope to find
          Salve for my body, and my mind.
Verse.   In Gilead though no balme be found,
          To ease this smart, or cure this wound ;
Ver. Chor. Yet, Lord, I know there is with Thee
          All saving health, and help for me.

Verse. Then reach Thou forth that hand of Thine,
   That powres in oyle, as well as wine.
Ver. Chor. And let it work, for I'le endure
   The utmost smart, so Thou wilt cure.

UPON GOD

GOD is all fore-part ; for, we never see
Any part backward in the Deitie.

CALLING, AND CORRECTING

GOD is not onely mercifull, to call
Men to repent, but when He strikes withall.

NO ESCAPING THE SCOURGING

GOD scourgeth some severely, some He spares ;
But all in smart have lesse, or greater shares.

THE ROD

GODS rod doth watch while men do sleep ; and then
The rod doth sleep, while vigilant are men.

GOD HAS A TWOFOLD PART

GOD when for sin He makes His children smart,
His own He acts not, but anothers part :
But when by stripes He saves them, then 'tis known,
He comes to play the part that is His own.

GOD IS ONE

GOD, as He is most holy knowne ;
So He is said to be most one.

PERSECUTIONS PROFITABLE

AFFLICTIONS they most profitable are
To the beholder, and the sufferer :
Bettering them both, but by a double straine,
The first by patience, and the last by paine.

TO GOD

Do with me, God ! as Thou didst deal with John,
(Who writ that heavenly Revelation) ;
Let me, like him, first cracks of thunder heare ;
Then let the harps inchantments strike mine eare ;
Here give me thornes ; there, in Thy kingdome, set
Upon my head the golden coronet ;
There give me day ; but here my dreadfull night :
My sackcloth here ; but there my stole of white.

WHIPS

GOD has His whips here to a twofold end,
The bad to punish, and the good t'amend.

GOD'S PROVIDENCE

IF all transgressions here should have their pay,
What need there then be of a reckning day :
If God should punish no sin, here, of men,
His providence who would not question then ?

TEMPTATION

THOSE saints, which God loves best,
The devill tempts not least.

HIS EJACULATION TO GOD

MY God! look on me with Thine eye
Of pittie, not of scrutinie;
For if Thou dost, Thou then shalt see
Nothing but loathsome sores in mee.
O then! for mercies sake, behold
These my irruptions manifold;
And heale me with Thy looke, or touch:
But if Thou wilt not deigne so much,
Because I'm odious in Thy sight,
Speak but the word, and cure me quite.

GODS GIFTS NOT SOONE GRANTED

GOD heares us when we pray, but yet defers
His gifts, to exercise petitioners:
And though a while He makes requesters stay,
With princely hand He'l recompence delay.

PERSECUTIONS PURIFIE

GOD strikes His church, but 'tis to this intent,
To make, not marre her, by this punishment:
So where He gives the bitter pills, be sure,
'Tis not to poyson, but to make thee pure.

PARDON

GOD pardons those, who do through frailty sin ;
But never those that persevere therein.

AN ODE OF THE BIRTH OF OUR SAVIOUR

IN numbers, and but these few,
I sing Thy birth, oh JESU !
Thou prettie babie, borne here,
With sup'rabundant scorn here :
Who for Thy princely port here,
Hadst for Thy place
Of birth, a base
Out-stable for Thy court here.

Instead of neat inclosures
Of inter-woven osiers ;
Instead of fragrant posies
Of daffadills, and roses ;
Thy cradle, kingly stranger,
As gospell tells,
Was nothing els,
But, here, a homely manger.

But we with silks, not cruells,
With sundry precious jewells,
And lilly-work will dresse Thee ;
And as we dispossesse Thee
Of clouts, wee'l make a chamber,
Sweet babe, for Thee,
Of ivorie,
And plaister'd round with amber.

The Jewes they did disdaine Thee,
But we will entertaine Thee
With glories to await here
Upon Thy princely state here,
And more for love, then pittie.
   From yeere to yeere
   Wee'l make Thee, here,
A free-born of our citie.

LIP-LABOUR

In the old Scripture I have often read,
The calfe without meale n'ere was offered ;
To figure to us, nothing more then this,
Without the heart, lip-labour nothing is.

THE HEART

In prayer the lips ne're act the winning part,
Without the sweet concurrence of the heart.

EARE-RINGS

Why wore th' Egyptians jewells in the eare ?
But for to teach us, all the grace is there,
When we obey, by acting what we heare.

SIN SEEN

When once the sin has fully acted been,
Then is the horror of the trespasse seen.

UPON TIME

TIME was upon
The wing, to flie away ;
    And I cal'd on
Him but a while to stay ;
    But he'd be gone,
For ought that I could say.

He held out then,
A writing, as he went ;
    And askt me, when
False man would be content
    To pay agen,
What God and Nature lent.

    An houre-glasse,
In which were sands but few,
    As he did passe,
He shew'd, and told me too,
    Mine end near was,
And so away he flew.

HIS PETITION

IF warre, or want shall make me grow so poore,
As for to beg my bread from doore to doore ;
Lord ! let me never act that beggars part,
Who hath Thee in his mouth, not in his heart.
He who asks almes in that so sacred Name,
Without due reverence, playes the cheaters game.

TO GOD

Thou hast promis'd, Lord, to be
With me in my miserie ;
Suffer me to be so bold,
As to speak, Lord, say and hold.

HIS LETANIE, TO THE HOLY SPIRIT

In the houre of my distresse,
When temptations me oppresse,
And when I my sins confesse,
    Sweet Spirit, comfort me !

When I lie within my bed,
Sick in heart, and sick in head,
And with doubts discomforted,
    Sweet Spirit, comfort me !

When the house doth sigh and weep,
And the world is drown'd in sleep,
Yet mine eyes the watch do keep ;
    Sweet Spirit, comfort me !

When the artlesse doctor sees
No one hope, but of his fees,
And his skill runs on the lees ;
    Sweet Spirit, comfort me !

When his potion and his pill,
His, or none, or little skill,
Meet for nothing, but to kill ;
    Sweet Spirit, comfort me !

When the passing-bell doth tole,
And the furies in a shole
Come to fright a parting soule ;
    Sweet Spirit, comfort me !

When the tapers now burne blew,
And the comforters are few,
And that number more then true ;
        Sweet Spirit, comfort me !

When the priest his last hath praid,
And I nod to what is said,
'Cause my speech is now decaid ;
        Sweet Spirit, comfort me !

When, God knowes, I'm tost about,
Either with despaire, or doubt ;
Yet before the glasse be out,
        Sweet Spirit, comfort me !

When the tempter me pursu'th
With the sins of all my youth,
And halfe damns me with untruth ;
        Sweet Spirit, comfort me !

When the flames and hellish cries
Fright mine eares, and fright mine eyes,
And all terrors me surprize ;
        Sweet Spirit, comfort me !

When the judgment is reveal'd,
And that open'd which was seal'd,
When to Thee I have appeal'd ;
        Sweet Spirit, comfort me !

THANKSGIVING

THANKSGIVING for a former, doth invite
God to bestow a second benefit.

COCK-CROW

BELL-MAN of night, if I about shall go
For to denie my Master, do thou crow.
Thou stop'st S. Peter in the midst of sin ;
Stay me, by crowing, ere I do begin ;
Better it is, premonish'd, for to shun
A sin, then fall to weeping when 'tis done.

ALL THINGS RUN WELL FOR THE RIGHTEOUS

ADVERSE and prosperous fortunes both work on
Here, for the righteous mans salvation :
Be he oppos'd, or be he not withstood,
All serve to th' augmentation of his good.

PAINE ENDS IN PLEASURE

AFFLICTIONS bring us joy in times to come,
When sins, by stripes, to us grow wearisome.

TO GOD

I'LE come, I'le creep, though Thou dost threat
Humbly unto Thy mercy-seat :
When I am there, this then I'le do,
Give Thee a dart, and dagger too ;
Next, when I have my faults confest,
Naked I'le shew a sighing brest ;
Which if that can't Thy pittie wooe,
Then let Thy justice do the rest,
                    And strike it through.

A THANKSGIVING TO GOD, FOR HIS
HOUSE

LORD, Thou hast given me a cell
   Wherein to dwell :
A little house, whose humble roof
   Is weather-proof ;
Under the sparres of which I lie
   Both soft, and drie ;
Where Thou my chamber for to ward
   Hast set a guard
Of harmlesse thoughts, to watch and keep
   Me, while I sleep.
Low is my porch, as is my fate,
   Both void of state ;
And yet the threshold of my doore
   Is worn by th' poore,
Who thither come, and freely get
   Good words, or meat :
Like as my parlour, so my hall
   And kitchin's small :
A little butterie, and therein
   A little byn,
Which keeps my little loafe of bread
   Unchipt, unflead :
Some brittle sticks of thorne or briar
   Make me a fire,
Close by whose living coale I sit,
   And glow like it.
Lord, I confesse too, when I dine,
   The pulse is Thine,
And all those other bits, that bee
   There plac'd by Thee ;
The worts, the purslain, and the messe
   Of water-cresse,
Which of Thy kindnesse Thou hast sent ;
   And my content

Makes those, and my beloved beet,
    To be more sweet.
'Tis thou that crown'st my glittering hearth
    With guiltlesse mirth ;
And giv'st me wassaile bowles to drink,
    Spic'd to the brink.
Lord, 'tis Thy plenty-dropping hand,
    That soiles my land ;
And giv'st me, for my bushell sowne,
    Twice ten for one :
Thou mak'st my teeming hen to lay
    Her egg each day :
Besides my healthfull ewes to beare
    Me twins each yeare :
The while the conduits of my kine
    Run creame, for wine.
All these, and better Thou dost send
    Me, to this end,
That I should render, for my part,
    A thankfull heart ;
Which, fir'd with incense, I resigne,
    As wholly Thine ;
But the acceptance, that must be,
    My Christ, by Thee.

TO GOD

MAKE, make me Thine, my gracious God,
Or with Thy staffe, or with Thy rod ;
And be the blow too what it will,
Lord, I will kisse it, though it kill :
Beat me, bruise me, rack me, rend me,
Yet, in torments, I'le commend Thee :
Examine me with fire, and prove me
To the full, yet I will love Thee :
Nor shalt Thou give so deep a wound,
But I as patient will be found.

ANOTHER, TO GOD

Lord, do not beat me,
Since I do sob and crie,
And swowne away to die,
Ere Thou dost threat me.
Lord, do not scourge me,
If I by lies and oaths
Have soil'd my selfe, or cloaths,
But rather purge me.

NONE TRULY HAPPY HERE

Happy's that man, to whom God gives
A stock of goods, whereby he lives
Neer to the wishes of his heart :
No man is blest through ev'ry part.

TO HIS EVER-LOVING GOD

Can I not come to Thee, my God, for these
So very-many-meeting hindrances,
That slack my pace ; but yet not make me stay ?
Who slowly goes, rids (in the end) his way.
Cleere Thou my paths, or shorten Thou my miles.
Remove the barrs, or lift me o're the stiles :
Since rough the way is, help me when I call,
And take me up ; or els prevent the fall.
I kenn my home ; and it affords some ease,
To see far off the smoaking villages.
Fain would I rest ; yet covet not to die,
For feare of future-biting penurie :
No, no, my God, Thou know'st my wishes be
To leave this life, not loving it, but Thee.

ANOTHER

THOU bidst me come ; I cannot come ; for why,
Thou dwel'st aloft, and I want wings to flie.
To mount my soule, she must have pineons given :
For, 'tis no easie way from earth to heaven.

TO DEATH

THOU bidst me come away,
And I'le no longer stay,
Then for to shed some teares
For faults of former yeares ;
And to repent some crimes,
Done in the present times :
And next, to take a bit
Of bread, and wine with it :
To d'on my robes of love,
Fit for the place above ;
To gird my loynes about
With charity throughout ;
And so to travaile hence
With feet of innocence :
These done, I'le onely crie
God mercy ; and so die.

NEUTRALITY LOATHSOME

GOD will have all, or none ; serve Him, or fall
Down before Baal, Bel, or Belial :
Either be hot, or cold : God doth despise,
Abhorre, and spew out all neutralities.

WELCOME WHAT COMES

WHATEVER comes, let's be content withall :
Among God's blessings, there is no one small.

TO HIS ANGRIE GOD

THROUGH all the night
Thou dost me fright,
And hold'st mine eyes from sleeping ;
And day, by day,
My cup can say,
My wine is mixt with weeping.

Thou dost my bread
With ashes knead,
Each evening and each morrow :
Mine eye and eare
Do see, and heare
The coming in of sorrow.

Thy scourge of steele,
Ay me ! I feele,
Upon me beating ever :
While my sick heart
With dismall smart
Is disacquainted never.

Long, long, I'm sure,
This can't endure ;
But in short time 'twill please Thee,
My gentle God,
To burn the rod,
Or strike so as to ease me.

PATIENCE, OR COMFORTS IN CROSSES

ABUNDANT plagues I late have had,
Yet none of these have made me sad :
For why, my Saviour, with the sense
Of suffring, gives me patience.

ETERNITIE

O YEARES! and age! farewell:
      Behold I go,
      Where I do know
Infinitie to dwell.

And these mine eyes shall see
      All times, how they
      Are lost i'th' sea
Of vast eternitie.

Where never moone shall sway
      The starres; but she,
      And night, shall be
Drown'd in one endlesse day.

TO HIS SAVIOUR, A CHILD; A PRESENT, BY A CHILD

Go, prettie child, and beare this flower
Unto thy little Saviour;
And tell Him, by that bud now blown,
He is the Rose of Sharon known:
When thou hast said so, stick it there
Upon His bibb, or stomacher:
And tell Him, for good handsell too,
That thou hast brought a whistle new,
Made of a clean strait oaten reed,
To charme His cries, at time of need:
Tell him, for corall, thou hast none;
But if thou had'st, He sho'd have one;
But poore thou art, and knowne to be
Even as monilesse, as He.
Lastly, if thou canst win a kisse
From those mellifluous lips of His;
Then never take a second on,
To spoile the first impression.

THE NEW-YEERES GIFT

LET others look for pearle and gold,
Tissues, or tabbies manifold :
One onely lock of that sweet hay
Whereon the blessed babie lay,
Or one poore swadling-clout, shall be
The richest new-yeeres gift to me.

TO GOD

IF any thing delight me for to print
My book, 'tis this ; that Thou, my God, art in't.

GOD, AND THE KING

How am I bound to two ! God, who doth give
The mind ; the king, the meanes whereby I live.

GODS MIRTH, MAN'S MOURNING

WHERE God is merry, there write down thy fears :
What He with laughter speaks, heare thou with tears.

HONOURS ARE HINDRANCES

GIVE me honours : what are these,
But the pleasing hindrances ?
Stiles, and stops, and stayes, that come
In the way 'twixt me, and home :
Cleer the walk, and then shall I
To my heaven lesse run, then flie.

THE PARASCEVE, OR PREPARATION

To a love-feast we both invited are :
The figur'd damask, or pure diaper,
Over the golden altar now is spread,
With bread, and wine, and vessells furnished ;
The sacred towell, and the holy eure
Are ready by, to make the guests all pure :
Let's go, my Alma, yet, e're we receive,
Fit, fit it is, we have our Parasceve.
Who to that sweet bread unprepar'd doth come,
Better he starv'd, then but to tast one crumme.

TO GOD

God gives not onely corne, for need,
But likewise sup'rabundant seed ;
Bread for our service, bread for shew ;
Meat for our meales, and fragments too :
He gives not poorly, taking some
Between the finger, and the thumb ;
But, for our glut, and for our store,
Fine flowre prest down, and running o're.

A WILL TO BE WORKING

Although we cannot turne the fervent fit
Of sin, we must strive 'gainst the streame of it ·
And howsoe're we have the conquest mist ;
'Tis for our glory, that we did resist.

CHRISTS PART

Christ, He requires still, wheresoere He comes,
To feed, or lodge, to have the best of roomes :
Give Him the choice ; grant Him the nobler part
Of all the house : the best of all's the heart.

RICHES AND POVERTY

God co'd have made all rich, or all men poore ;
But why He did not, let me tell wherefore :
Had all been rich, where then had patience been ?
Had all been poore, who had His bounty seen ?

SOBRIETY IN SEARCH

To seek of God more then we well can find,
Argues a strong distemper of the mind.

ALMES

Give, if thou canst, an almes ; if not, afford,
Instead of that, a sweet and gentle word :
God crowns our goodnesse, wheresoere He sees,
On our part, wanting all abilities.

TO HIS CONSCIENCE

Can I not sin, but thou wilt be
My private protonotarie ?
Can I not wooe thee to passe by
A short and sweet iniquity ?
I'le cast a mist and cloud, upon
My delicate transgression,
So utter dark, as that no eye
Shall see the hug'd impietie :
Gifts blind the wise, and bribes do please,
And winde all other witnesses :
And wilt not thou, with gold, be ti'd
To lay thy pen and ink aside ?

That in the mirk and tonguelesse night,
Wanton I may, and thou not write?
It will not be: and, therefore, now,
For times to come, I'le make this vow,
From aberrations to live free;
So I'le not feare the Judge, or thee.

TO HIS SAVIOUR

LORD, I confesse, that Thou alone art able
To purifie this my Augean stable:
Be the seas water, and the land all sope,
Yet if Thy bloud not wash me, there's no hope.

TO GOD

GOD is all-sufferance here; here He doth show
No arrow nockt, onely a stringlesse bow:
His arrowes flie; and all his stones are hurl'd
Against the wicked, in another world.

HIS DREAME

I DREAMT, last night, Thou didst transfuse
Oyle from Thy jarre, into my creuze;
And powring still, Thy wealthy store,
The vessell full, did then run ore:
Me thought, I did Thy bounty chide,
To see the waste; but 'twas repli'd
By Thee, deare God, God gives man seed
Oft-times for wast, as for his need.
Then I co'd say, that house is bare,
That has not bread, and some to spare.

GODS BOUNTY

GODS bounty, that ebbs lesse and lesse,
As men do wane in thankfulnesse.

TO HIS SWEET SAVIOUR

NIGHT hath no wings, to him that cannot sleep ;
And Time seems then, not for to flie, but creep ;
Slowly her chariot drives, as if that she
Had broke her wheele, or crackt her axeltree.
Just so it is with me, who list'ning, pray
The winds, to blow the tedious night away ;
That I might see the cheerfull peeping day.
Sick is my heart ! O Saviour ! do Thou please
To make my bed soft in my sicknesses :
Lighten my candle, so that I beneath
Sleep not for ever in the vaults of death :
Let me Thy voice betimes i'th' morning heare ;
Call, and I'le come ; say Thou, the when, and where :
Draw me, but first, and after Thee I'le run,
And make no one stop, till my race be done.

HIS CREED

I DO believe, that die I must,
And be return'd from out my dust :
I do believe, that when I rise,
Christ I shall see, with these same eyes :
I do believe, that I must come,
With others, to the dreadfull doome :
I do believe, the bad must goe
From thence, to everlasting woe :
I do believe, the good, and I,

Shall live with Him eternally :
I do believe, I shall inherit
Heaven, by Christs mercies, not my merit :
I do believe, the One in Three,
And Three in perfect Unitie :
Lastly, that JESUS is a deed
Of gift from God : and heres my creed.

TEMPTATIONS

TEMPTATIONS hurt not, though they have accesse :
Satan o'ercomes none, but by willingnesse.

THE LAMP

WHEN a man's faith is frozen up, as dead ;
Then is the lamp and oyle extinguished.

SORROWES

SORROWES our portion are : ere hence we goe,
Crosses we must have ; or, hereafter woe.

PENITENCIE

A MANS transgressions God do's then remit,
When man he makes a penitent for it.

THE DIRGE OF JEPHTHAH'S DAUGHTER

SUNG BY THE VIRGINS

O THOU, the wonder of all dayes !
O paragon, and pearle of praise !

O Virgin-martyr, ever blest
     Above the rest
Of all the maiden-traine ! We come,
And bring fresh strewings to thy tombe.

Thus, thus, and thus we compasse round
Thy harmlesse and unhaunted ground ;
And as we sing thy dirge, we will
     The dafadill,
And other flowers, lay upon
(The altar of our love) thy stone.

Thou wonder of all maids, li'st here,
Of daughters all, the deerest deere ;
The eye of virgins ; nay, the queen
     Of this smooth green,
And all sweete meades ; from whence we get
The primrose, and the violet.

Too soon, too deere did Jephthah buy,
By thy sad losse, our liberty :
His was the bond and cov'nant, yet
     Thou paid'st the debt,
Lamented maid ! he won the day,
But for the conquest thou didst pay.

Thy father brought with him along
The olive branch, and victors song :
He slew the Ammonites, we know,
     But to thy woe ;
And in the purchase of our peace,
The cure was worse than the disease.

For which obedient zeale of thine,
We offer here, before thy shrine,
Our sighs for storax, teares for wine ;
     And to make fine,

And fresh thy herse-cloth, we will, here,
Foure times bestrew thee ev'ry yeere.

Receive, for this thy praise, our teares :
Receive this offering of our haires :
Receive these christall vialls fil'd
                With teares, distil'd
From teeming eyes ; to these we bring,
Each maid, her silver filleting,

To guild thy tombe ; besides, these caules,
These laces, ribbands, and these faules,
These veiles, wherewith we use to hide
                The bashfull bride,
When we conduct her to her groome :
And, all we lay upon thy tombe.

No more, no more, since thou art dead,
Shall we ere bring coy brides to bed ;
No more, at yeerly festivalls
                We cowslip balls,
Or chaines of columbines shall make,
For this, or that occasions sake.

No, no ; our maiden-pleasures be
Wrapt in the winding-sheet, with thee :
'Tis we are dead, though not i'th' grave :
                Or, if we have
One seed of life left, 'tis to keep
A Lent for thee, to fast and weep.

Sleep in thy peace, thy bed of spice ;
And make this place all paradise :
May sweets grow here ! & smoke from hence
                Fat frankincense :
Let balme, and cassia send their scent
From out thy maiden-monument.

May no wolfe howle, or screech-owle stir
A wing about thy sepulcher !
No boysterous winds, or stormes, come hither,
         To starve, or wither
Thy soft sweet earth ! but, like a spring,
Love keep it ever flourishing.

May all shie maids, at wonted hours,
Come forth, to strew thy tombe with flow'rs :
May virgins, when they come to mourn,
         Male-incense burn
Upon thine altar ! then return,
And leave thee sleeping in thy urn.

TO GOD, ON HIS SICKNESSE

WHAT though my harp, and violl be
Both hung upon the willow-tree ?
What though my bed be now my grave,
And for my house I darknesse have ?
What though my healthfull dayes are fled,
And I lie numbred with the dead ?
Yet I have hope, by Thy great power,
  To spring ; though now a wither'd flower.

SINS LOATH'D, AND YET LOV'D

SHAME checks our first attempts ; but then 'tis prov'd,
Sins first dislik'd, are after that belov'd.

SIN

SIN leads the way, but as it goes, it feels
The following plague still treading on his heels.

UPON GOD

GOD when He takes my goods and chattels hence,
Gives me a portion, giving patience :
What is in God is God ; if so it be,
He patience gives ; He gives Himselfe to me.

FAITH

WHAT here we hope for, we shall once inherit :
By faith we all walk here, not by the spirit.

HUMILITY

HUMBLE we must be, if to heaven we go :
High is the roof there ; but the gate is low :
When e're thou speak'st, look with a lowly eye :
Grace is increased by humility.

TEARES

OUR present teares here, not our present laughter,
Are but the handsells of our joyes hereafter.

SIN AND STRIFE

AFTER true sorrow for our sinnes, our strife
Must last with Satan, to the end of life.

AN ODE, OR PSALME, TO GOD

DEER God,
If Thy smart rod
Here did not make me sorrie,

                    I sho'd not be
                    With Thine, or Thee,
              In Thy eternall glorie.

                    But since
                    Thou didst convince
              My sinnes, by gently striking ;
                    Add still to those
                    First stripes, new blowes,
              According to Thy liking.

                    . Feare me,
                    Or scourging teare me ;
              That thus from vices driven,
                    I may from hell
                    Flie up, to dwell
              With Thee· and Thine in heaven.

GRACES FOR CHILDREN

WHAT God gives, and what we take,
'Tis a gift for Christ His sake :
Be the meale of beanes and pease,
God be thank'd for those, and these :
Have we flesh, or have we fish,
All are fragments from His dish.
He His church save, and the king,
And our peace here, like a spring,
Make it ever flourishing.

GOD TO BE FIRST SERV'D

HONOUR thy parents ; but good manners call
Thee to adore thy God, the first of all.

ANOTHER GRACE FOR A CHILD

HERE a little child I stand,
Heaving up my either hand :
Cold as paddocks though they be,
Here I lift them up to Thee,
For a benizon to fall
On our meat, and on us all.   Amen.

A CHRISTMAS CAROLL

SUNG TO THE KING IN THE PRESENCE AT WHITE-HALL

Chor. WHAT sweeter musick can we bring,
Then a caroll, for to sing
The birth of this our heavenly King ?
Awake the voice ! awake the string !
Heart, eare, and eye, and every thing
Awake ! the while the active finger
Runs division with the singer.

From the flourish they came to the song

1 Dark and dull night, flie hence away,
And give the honour to this day,
That sees December turn'd to May.

2 If we may ask the reason, say ;
The why, and wherefore all things here
Seem like the spring-time of the yeere ?

3 Why do's the chilling winters morne
Smile, like a field beset with corne ?
Or smell, like to a meade new-shorne,

Thus, on the sudden ?   4. Come and see
The cause, why things thus fragrant be :
'Tis He is borne, whose quickning birth
Gives life and luster, publike mirth,
To heaven, and the under-earth.

Chor. We see Him come, and know Him ours,
Who, with His sun-shine, and His showers,
Turnes all the patient ground to flowers.

1 The darling of the world is come,
And fit it is, we finde a roome
To welcome Him.   2. The nobler part
Of all the house here, is the heart,

Chor. Which we will give Him ; and bequeath
This hollie, and this ivie wreath,
To do Him honour ; who's our King,
And Lord of all this revelling.
The musicall part was composed by
M. Henry Lawes.

THE NEW-YEERES GIFT, or CIRCUMCISIONS SONG

SUNG TO THE KING IN THE PRESENCE AT WHITE-HALL

1 PREPARE for songs ; He's come, He's come ;
And be it sin here to be dumb,
And not with lutes to fill the roome.

2 Cast holy water all about,
And have a care no fire gos out,
But 'cense the porch, and place throughout.

3 The altars all on fier be ;
   The storax fries ; and ye may see,
   How heart and hand do all agree,
To make things sweet. *Chor.* Yet all less sweet
     then He.

4 Bring Him along, most pious priest,
   And tell us then, when as thou seest
   His gently-gliding, dove-like eyes,
   And hear'st His whimp'ring, and His cries ;
   How canst thou this babe circumcise ?

5 Ye must not be more pitifull then wise ;
   For, now unlesse ye see Him bleed,
   Which makes the bapti'me ; 'tis decreed,
The birth is fruitlesse : *Chor.* Then the work God
     speed.

1 Touch gently, gently touch ; and here
   Spring tulips up through all the yeere ;
   And from His sacred bloud, here shed,
May roses grow, to crown His own deare head.

Chor. Back, back again ; each thing is done
   With zeale alike, as 'twas begun ;

   Now singing, homeward let us carrie
   The babe unto His mother Marie ;
   And when we have the child commended
To her warm bosome, then our rites are ended.
         Composed by M. Henry Lawes.

ANOTHER NEW-YEERES GIFT, or SONG FOR THE CIRCUMCISION

1 HENCE, hence, prophane, and none appeare
   With any thing unhallowed, here :
   No jot of leven must be found
   Conceal'd in this most holy ground :

2 What is corrupt, or sowr'd with sin,
Leave that without, then enter in ;

Chor. But let no Christmas mirth begin
Before ye purge, and circumcise
Your hearts, and hands, lips, eares, and eyes.

3 Then, like a perfum'd altar, see
That all things sweet, and clean may be :
For, here's a babe, that, like a bride,
Will blush to death, if ought be spi'd
Ill-scenting, or unpurifi'd.

Chor. The room is 'censed : help, help t'invoke
Heaven to come down, the while we choke
The temple, with a cloud of smoke.

4 Come then, and gently touch the birth
Of Him, who's Lord of heav'n and earth ;

5 And softly handle Him : y'ad need,
Because the prettie babe do's bleed.
Poore-pittied child ! who from Thy stall
Bring'st in Thy blood, a balm, that shall
Be the best new-yeares gift to all.

1 Let's bless the babe : and, as we sing
His praise ; so let us blesse the King :

Chor. Long may He live, till He hath told
His new-yeeres trebled to His old :
And, when that's done, to re-aspire
A new-borne Phœnix from His own chast fire.

GODS PARDON

WHEN I shall sin, pardon my trespasse here ;
For, once in hell, none knowes remission there.

SIN

Sin once reacht up to Gods eternall sphere,
And was committed, not remitted there.

EVILL

Evill no nature hath ; the losse of good
Is that which gives to sin a livelihood.

THE STAR-SONG

A CAROLL TO THE KING ; SUNG AT WHITE-HALL

The flourish of musick : then followed the song

1 Tell us, thou cleere and heavenly tongue,
Where is the babe but lately sprung ?
Lies He the lillie-banks among ?

2 Or say, if this new birth of ours
Sleeps, laid within some ark of flowers,
Spangled with deaw-light ; thou canst cleere
All doubts, and manifest the where.

3 Declare to us, bright Star, if we shall seek
Him in the mornings blushing cheek,
Or search the beds of spices through,
To find Him out ?
Star. No, this ye need not do ;
But only come, and see Him rest
A princely babe in's mothers brest.

Chor. He's seen, He's seen, why then a round,
Let's kisse the sweet and holy ground ;
And all rejoyce, that we have found
A King, before conception crown'd.

4 Come then, come then, and let us bring
  Unto our prettie Twelfth-Tide King,
  Each one his severall offering ;

Chor. And when night comes, wee'l give Him was-
        sailing :
And that His treble honours may be seen,
Wee'l chuse Him King, and make His mother queen.

TO GOD

WITH golden censers, and with incense, here,
Before Thy virgin-altar I appeare,
To pay Thee that I owe, since what I see
In, or without ; all, all belongs to Thee :
Where shall I now begin to make, for one
Least loane of Thine, half restitution ?
Alas ! I cannot pay a jot ; therefore
I'le kisse the tally, and confesse the score.
Ten thousand talents lent me, Thou dost write :
'Tis true, my God ; *but I can't pay one mite.*

TO HIS DEERE GOD

I'LE hope no more,
  For things that will not come :
And, if they do, they prove but cumbersome ;
    Wealth brings much woe :
    And, since it fortunes so ;
  'Tis better to be poore,
    Than so t'abound,
    As to be drown'd,
  Or overwhelm'd with store.

Pale care, avant,
I'le learn to be content
With that small stock, Thy bounty gave or lent.
What may conduce
To my most healthfull use,
Almighty God, me grant ;
But that, or this,
That hurtfull is,
Denie Thy suppliant.

TO GOD, HIS GOOD WILL

GOLD I have none, but I present my need,
O Thou, that crown'st the will, where wants the deed.
Where rams are wanting, or large bullocks thighs,
There a poor lamb's a plenteous sacrifice.
Take then his vowes, who, if he had it, would
Devote to Thee, both incense, myrrhe, and gold,
Upon an altar rear'd by him, and crown'd
Both with the rubie, pearle, and diamond.

ON HEAVEN

PERMIT mine eyes to see
Part, or the whole of Thee,
O happy place !
Where all have grace,
And garlands shar'd,
For their reward ;
Where each chast soule
In long white stole,
And palmes in hand,
Do ravisht stand ;
So in a ring,
The praises sing

Of Three in One,
That fill the throne ;
While harps, and violls then
To voices, say, Amen.

THE SUMME, AND THE SATISFACTION

LAST night I drew up mine account,
And found my debits to amount
To such a height, as for to tell
How I sho'd pay, 's impossible :
Well, this I'le do ; my mighty score
Thy mercy-seat I'le lay before ;
But therewithall I'le bring the band,
Which, in full force, did daring stand,
Till my Redeemer, on the tree,
Made void for millions, as for me.
Then, if Thou bidst me pay, or go
Unto the prison, I'le say, no ;
Christ having paid, I nothing owe :
For, this is sure, the debt is dead
By law, the bond once cancelled.

GOOD MEN AFFLICTED MOST

GOD makes not good men wantons, but doth bring
Them to the field, and, there, to skirmishing ;
With trialls those, with terrors these He proves,
And hazards those most, whom the most He loves ;
For Sceva, darts ; for Cocles, dangers ; thus
He finds a fire for mighty Mutius ;
Death for stout Cato ; and besides all these,
A poyson too He has for Socrates ;
Torments for high Attilius ; and, with want,
Brings in Fabricius for a combatant :
But, bastard-slips, and such as He dislikes,
He never brings them once to th' push of pikes.

GOOD CHRISTIANS

PLAY their offensive and defensive parts,
Till they be hid o're with a wood of darts.

THE WILL THE CAUSE OF WOE

WHEN man is punisht, he is plagued still,
Not for the fault of Nature, but of will.

TO HEAVEN

OPEN thy gates
To him, who weeping waits,
    And might come in,
But that held back by sin.
    Let mercy be
So kind, to set me free,
    And I will strait
Come in, or force the gate.

THE RECOMPENCE

ALL I have lost, that co'd be rapt from me ;
And fare it well : yet, Herrick, if so be
Thy deerest Saviour renders thee but one
Smile, that one smile's full restitution.

TO GOD

PARDON me God, once more I Thee intreat,
That I have plac'd Thee in so meane a seat,

Where round about Thou seest but all things vaine.
Uncircumcis'd, unseason'd, and prophane.
But as heavens publike and immortall eye
Looks on the filth, but is not soil'd thereby ;
So Thou, my God, may'st on this impure look,
But take no tincture from my sinfull book :
Let but one beame of glory on it shine,
And that will make me, and my work divine.

TO GOD

LORD, I am like to misletoe,
Which has no root, and cannot grow,
Or prosper, but by that same tree
It clings about ; so I by Thee.
What need I then to feare at all,
So long as I about Thee craule ?
But if that Tree sho'd fall, and die,
Tumble shall heav'n, and down will I.

HIS WISH TO GOD

I WOULD to God, that mine old age might have
Before my last, but here a living grave,
Some one poore almes-house ; there to lie, or stir,
Ghost-like, as in my meaner sepulcher ;
A little piggin, and a pipkin by,
To hold things fitting my necessity ;
Which, rightly us'd, both in their time and place,
Might me excite to fore, and after-grace.
Thy crosse, my Christ, fixt 'fore mine eyes sho'd be,
Not to adore that, but to worship Thee.
So, here the remnant of my dayes I'd spend,
Reading Thy Bible, and my book ; so end.

SATAN

WHEN we 'gainst Satan stoutly fight, the more
He teares and tugs us, then he did before ;
Neglecting once to cast a frown on those
Whom ease makes his, without the help of blowes.

HELL

HELL is no other but a soundlesse pit,
Where no one beame of comfort peeps in it.

THE WAY

WHEN I a ship see on the seas,
Cuft with those watrie savages,
And therewithall, behold, it hath
In all that way no beaten path ;
Then, with a wonder, I confesse,
Thou art our way i'th wildernesse :
And while we blunder in the dark,
Thou art our candle there, or spark.

GREAT GRIEF, GREAT GLORY

THE lesse our sorrowes here and suffrings cease,
The more our crownes of glory there increase.

HELL

HELL is the place where whipping-cheer abounds,
But no one jailor there to wash the wounds.

THE BELL-MAN

ALONG the dark, and silent night,
With my lantern, and my light,
And the tinkling of my bell,
Thus I walk, and this I tell :
Death and dreadfulnesse call on,
To the gen'rall session ;
To whose dismall barre, we there
All accompts must come to cleere :
Scores of sins w'ave made here many,
Wip't out few, God knowes, if any.
Rise, ye debters, then, and fall
To make paiment, while I call.
Ponder this, when I am gone ;
By the clock 'tis almost one.

THE GOODNESSE OF HIS GOD

WHEN winds and seas do rage,
    And threaten to undo me,
Thou dost their wrath asswage,
    If I but call unto Thee.

A mighty storm last night
    Did seek my soule to swallow
But by the peep of light
    A gentle calme did follow.

What need I then despaire,
    Though ills stand round about me ;
Since mischiefs neither dare
    To bark, or bite, without Thee ?

THE WIDOWES TEARES: OR, DIRGE OF DORCAS

COME pitie us, all ye, who see
Our harps hung on the willow-tree:
Come pitie us, ye passers by,
Who see, or heare poor widdowes crie:
Come pitie us; and bring your eares,
And eyes, to pitie widdowes teares.
    Chor. And when you are come hither;
        Then we will keep
        A fast, and weep
    Our eyes out all together.

For Tabitha, who dead lies here,
Clean washt, and laid out for the beere;
O modest matrons, weep and waile!
For now the corne and wine must faile:
The basket and the bynn of bread,
Wherewith so many soules were fed.
    Chor. Stand empty here for ever:
        And ah! the pore,
        At thy worne doore,
    Shall be releeved never.

Woe worth the time, woe worth the day,
That reav'd us of thee, Tabitha!
For we have lost, with thee, the meale,
The bits, the morsells, and the deale
Of gentle paste, and yeelding dow,
That thou on widdowes didst bestow.
    Chor. All's gone, and Death hath taken
        Away from us
        Our maundie; thus,
    Thy widdowes stand forsaken.

Ah Dorcas, Dorcas ! now adieu
We bid the creuse and pannier too :
I and the flesh, for and the fish,
Dol'd to us in that lordly dish.
We take our leaves now of the loome,
From whence the house-wives cloth did come :
    Chor. The web affords now nothing ;
           Thou being dead,
           The woosted thred
       Is cut, that made us clothing.

Farewell the flax and reaming wooll,
With which thy house was plentifull.
Farewell the coats, the garments, and
The sheets, the rugs, made by thy hand.
Farewell thy fier and thy light,
That ne're went out by day or night :
    Chor. No, or thy zeale so speedy,
           That found a way
           By peep of day
       To feed and cloth the needy.

But, ah, alas ! the almond bough,
And olive branch is wither'd now.
The wine presse now is ta'ne from us,
The saffron and the calamus.
The spice and spiknard hence is gone,
The storax and the synamon,
      Chor. The caroll of our gladnesse
            Has taken wing,
            And our late spring
       Of mirth is turn'd to sadnesse.

How wise wast thou in all thy waies !
How worthy of respect and praise !
How matron-like didst thou go drest !
How soberly above the rest
Of those that prank it with their plumes ;

And jet it with their choice purfumes.
      Chor. Thy vestures were not flowing :
            Nor did the street
            Accuse thy feet
      Of mincing in their going.

And though thou here li'st dead, we see
A deale of beauty yet in thee.
How sweetly shewes thy smiling face,
Thy lips with all diffused grace !
Thy hands, though cold, yet spotlesse, white,
And comely as the chrysolite.
      Chor. Thy belly like a hill is,
            Or as a neat
            Cleane heap of wheat,
      All set about with lillies.

Sleep with thy beauties here, while we
Will shew these garments made by thee ;
These were the coats, in these are read
The monuments of Dorcas dead.
These were thy acts, and thou shalt have
These hung, as honours o're thy grave,
      Chor. And after us, distressed,
            Sho'd fame be dumb ;
            Thy very tomb
      Would cry out, Thou art blessed.

TO GOD, IN TIME OF PLUNDERING

RAPINE has yet tooke nought from me ;
But if it please my God, I be
Brought at the last to th' utmost bit,
God make me thankfull still for it.
I have been gratefull for my store :
Let me say grace when there's no more.

TO HIS SAVIOUR. THE NEW-YEERS GIFT

THAT little prettie bleeding part
    Of foreskin send to me :
And Ile returne a bleeding heart,
    For New-yeers gift to Thee.

Rich is the jemme that Thou didst send,
    Mine's faulty too, and small :
But yet this gift Thou wilt commend,
    Because I send Thee all.

DOOMES-DAY

LET not that day Gods friends and servants scare :
The bench is then their place ; and not the barre.

THE POORES PORTION

THE sup'rabundance of my store,
That is the portion of the poore :
Wheat, barley, rie, or oats ; what is't
But He takes tole of ? all the griest.
Two raiments have I : Christ then makes
This law ; that He and I part stakes.
Or have I two loaves ; then I use
The poore to cut, and I to chuse.

THE WHITE ISLAND : OR PLACE OF THE BLEST

IN this world, the Isle of Dreames,
While we sit by sorrowes streames,
Teares and terrors are our theames
        Reciting :

But when once from hence we flie,
More and more approaching nigh
Unto young Eternitie
                          Uniting :

In that whiter island, where
Things are evermore sincere ;
Candor here, and lustre there
                          Delighting :

There no monstrous fancies shall
Out of hell an horrour call,
To create, or cause at all,
                          Affrighting.

There in calm and cooling sleep
We our eyes shall never steep ;
But eternall watch shall keep,
                          Attending

Pleasures, such as shall pursue
Me immortaliz'd, and you ;
And fresh joyes, as never too
                          Have ending.

TO CHRIST

I CRAWLE, I creep ; my Christ, I come
To Thee, for curing balsamum :
Thou hast, nay more, Thou art the tree,
Affording salve of soveraigntie.
My mouth I'le lay unto Thy wound
Bleeding, that no blood touch the ground :
For, rather then one drop shall fall
To wast, my JESU, I'le take all.

TO GOD

God! to my little meale and oyle,
Add but a bit of flesh, to boyle:
And Thou my pipkinnet shalt see,
Give a wave-offring unto Thee.

FREE WELCOME

God He refuseth no man; but makes way
For all that now come, or hereafter may.

GODS GRACE

Gods Grace deserves here to be daily fed,
That, thus increast, it might be perfected.

COMING TO CHRIST

To him, who longs unto his Christ to go,
Celerity even it self is slow.

CORRECTION

God had but one Son free from sin; but none
Of all His sonnes free from correction.

GODS BOUNTY

God, as He's potent, so He's likewise known,
To give us more then hope can fix upon.

KNOWLEDGE

Science in God, is known to be
A substance, not a qualitie.

SALUTATION

Christ, I have read, did to His chaplains say,
Sending them forth, Salute no man by th' way:
Not, that He taught His ministers to be
Unsmooth, or sowre, to all civilitie ;
But to instruct them, to avoid all snares
Of tardidation in the Lords affaires.
Manners are good : but till his errand ends,
Salute we must, nor strangers, kin, or friends.

LASCIVIOUSNESSE

Lasciviousnesse is known to be
The sister to saturitie.

TEARES

God from our eyes all teares hereafter wipes,
And gives His children kisses then, not stripes.

GODS BLESSING

In vain our labours are, whatsoe're they be,
Unlesse God gives the Benedicite.

GOD, AND LORD

GOD, is His name of nature ; but that word
Implies His power, when He's cal'd the LORD.

THE JUDGMENT-DAY

GOD hides from man the reck'ning day, that He
May feare it ever for uncertaintie :
That being ignorant of that one, he may
Expect the coming of it ev'ry day.

ANGELLS

ANGELLS are called gods ; yet of them, none
Are gods, but by participation :
As just men are intitled gods, yet none
Are gods, of them, but by adoption.

LONG LIFE

THE longer thred of life we spin,
The more occasion still to sin.

TEARES

THE teares of saints more sweet by farre,
Then all the songs of sinners are.

MANNA

THAT manna, which God on His people cast,
Fitted it self to ev'ry feeders tast.

REVERENCE

TRUE rev'rence is, as Cassiodore doth prove,
The feare of God, commixt with cleanly love.

MERCY

MERCY, the wise Athenians held to be
Not an affection, but a deitie.

WAGES

AFTER this life, the wages shall
Not shar'd alike be unto all.

TEMPTATION

GOD tempteth no one, as S. Aug'stine saith,
For any ill ; but, for the proof of faith :
Unto temptation God exposeth some ;
But none, of purpose, to be overcome.

GODS HANDS

GODS hands are round, and smooth, that gifts may fall
Freely from them, and hold none back at all.

LABOUR

LABOUR we must, and labour hard
I'th forum here, or vineyard.

MORA SPONSI, THE STAY OF THE BRIDEGROOME

THE time the bridegroom stayes from hence,
Is but the time of penitence.

ROARING

ROARING is nothing but a weeping part,
Forc'd from the mighty dolour of the heart.

THE EUCHARIST

HE that is hurt seeks help : sin is the wound ;
The salve for this i'th Eucharist is found.

SIN SEVERELY PUNISHT

GOD in His own day will be then severe,
To punish great sins, who small faults whipt here.

MONTES SCRIPTURARUM, THE MOUNTS OF THE SCRIPTURES

THE mountains of the Scriptures are, some say,
Moses, and Jesus, called Joshua :
The Prophets mountains of the Old are meant ;
The Apostles mounts of the New Testament.

PRAYER

A PRAYER, that is said alone,
Starves, having no companion.
Great things ask for, when thou dost pray,
And those great are, which ne're decay.
Pray not for silver, rust eats this ;
Ask not for gold, which metall is :
Nor yet for houses, which are here
But earth : *such vowes nere reach Gods eare.*

CHRISTS SADNESSE

CHRIST was not sad, i'th garden, for His own
Passion, but for His sheeps dispersion.

GOD HEARES US

GOD, who's in Heav'n, will hear from thence ;
If not to'th sound, yet, to the sense.

GOD

GOD, as the learned Damascen doth write,
A Sea of Substance is, Indefinite.

CLOUDS

HE that ascended in a cloud, shall come
In clouds, descending to the publike doome.

COMFORTS IN CONTENTIONS

THE same, who crownes the conquerour, will be
A coadjutor in the agonie.

HEAVEN

HEAV'N is most faire ; but fairer He
That made that fairest canopie.

GOD

IN God there's nothing, but 'tis known to be
Ev'n God Himself, in perfect entitie.

HIS POWER

GOD can do all things, save but what are known
For to imply a contradiction.

CHRISTS WORDS ON THE CROSSE, MY GOD, MY GOD

CHRIST, when He hung the dreadfull crosse upon,
Had, as it were, a dereliction ;
In this regard, in those great terrors He
Had no one beame from Gods sweet majestie.

JEHOVAH

JEHOVAH, as Boëtius saith,
No number of the plurall hath.

CONFUSION OF FACE

GOD then confounds mans face, when He not hears
The vowes of those, who are petitioners.

ANOTHER

THE shame of man's face is no more
Then prayers repel'd, sayes Cassiodore.

BEGGARS

JACOB Gods beggar was ; and so we wait,
Though ne're so rich, all beggars at His gate.

GOOD, AND BAD

THE bad among the good are here mixt ever ;
The good without the bad are here plac'd never.

SIN

SIN no existence ; Nature none it hath,
Or good at all, as learn'd Aquinas saith.

MARTHA, MARTHA

THE repetition of the name made known
No other, then Christs full affection.

YOUTH, AND AGE

GOD on our youth bestowes but little ease :
But on our age most sweet indulgences.

GODS POWER

GOD is so potent, as His power can
Draw out of bad a soveraigne good to man.

PARADISE

PARADISE is, as from the learn'd I gather,
A quire of blest soules circling in the Father.

OBSERVATION

THE Jewes, when they built houses, I have read,
One part thereof left still unfinished :
To make them, thereby, mindfull of their own
Cities most sad and dire destruction.

THE ASSE

GOD did forbid the Israelites, to bring
An asse unto Him, for an offering :
Onely, by this dull creature, to expresse
His detestation to all slothfulnesse.

OBSERVATION

THE Virgin-Mother stood at distance there,
From her Sonnes crosse, not shedding once a teare :
Because the law forbad to sit and crie
For those, who did as malefactors die.
So she, to keep her mighty woes in awe,
Tortur'd her love, not to transgresse the law.
Observe we may, how Mary Joses then,
And th' other Mary, Mary Magdalen,
Sate by the grave ; and sadly sitting there,
Shed for their Master many a bitter teare :
But 'twas not till their dearest Lord was dead ;
And then to weep they both were licensed.

TAPERS

THOSE tapers, which we set upon the grave,
In fun'rall pomp, but this importance have ;
That soules departed are not put out quite ;
But, as they walk't here in their vestures white,
So live in Heaven, in everlasting light.

CHRISTS BIRTH

ONE birth our Saviour had ; the like none yet
Was, or will be a second like to it.

THE VIRGIN MARY

To work a wonder, God would have her shown,
At once, a bud, and yet a rose full-blowne.

ANOTHER

As sun-beames pierce the glasse, and streaming in,
No crack or schisme leave i'th subtill skin :
So the Divine Hand work't, and brake no thred,
But, in a mother, kept a maiden-head.

GOD

GOD, in the holy tongue, they call
The place that filleth All in all.

ANOTHER OF GOD

GOD'S said to leave this place, and for to come
Nearer to that place, then to other some :
Of locall motion, in no least respect,
But only by impression of effect.

ANOTHER

GOD is Jehovah cal'd ; which name of His
Implies or essence, or the He that Is.

GODS PRESENCE

GOD's evident, and may be said to be
Present with just men, to the veritie :
But with the wicked, if He doth comply,
'Tis, as S. Bernard saith, but seemingly.

GODS DWELLING

GOD's said to dwell there, wheresoever He
Puts down some prints of His high majestie :
As when to man He comes, and there doth place
His holy Spirit, or doth plant His grace.

THE VIRGIN MARY

THE Virgin Marie was, as I have read,
The House of God, by Christ inhabited ;
Into the which He enter'd : but, the doore
Once shut, was never to be opened more.

TO GOD

GOD's undivided, One in Persons Three ,
And Three in Inconfused Unity :
Originall of Essence there is none,
'Twixt God the Father, Holy Ghost, and Sonne :
And though the Father be the first of Three,
'Tis but by order, not by entitie.

UPON WOMAN AND MARY

So long, it seem'd, as Maries faith was small,
Christ did her woman, not her Mary call :
But no more woman, being strong in faith ;
But Mary cal'd then, as S. Ambrose saith.

NORTH AND SOUTH

The Jewes their beds, and offices of ease,
Plac't north and south, for these cleane purposes ;
That mans uncomely froth might not molest
Gods wayes and walks, which lie still east and west.

SABBATHS

Sabbaths are threefold, as S. Austine sayes :
The first of time, or Sabbath here of dayes ;
The second is a conscience trespasse-free ;
The last the Sabbath of Eternitie.

THE FAST, or LENT

Noah the first was, as tradition sayes,
That did ordaine the fast of forty dayes.

SIN

There is no evill that we do commit,
But hath th' extraction of some good from it :
As when we sin ; God, the great Chymist, thence
Drawes out th' elixar of true penitence.

GOD

GOD is more here, then in another place,
Not by His Essence, but commerce of grace.

THIS, AND THE NEXT WORLD

GOD hath this world for many made ; 'tis true :
But He hath made the world to come for few.

EASE

GOD gives to none so absolute an ease,
As not to know, or feel some grievances.

BEGINNINGS AND ENDINGS

PAUL, he began ill, but he ended well ;
Judas began well, but he foulely fell :
In godlinesse, not the beginnings, so
Much as the ends are to be lookt unto.

TEMPORALL GOODS

THESE temp'rall goods God, the most wise, commends
To th' good and bad, in common, for two ends :
First, that these goods none here may o're esteem,
Because the wicked do partake of them :
Next, that these ills none cowardly may shun ;
Being, oft here, the just mans portion.

HELL FIRE

THE fire of hell this strange condition hath,
To burn, not shine, as learned Basil saith.

ABELS BLOUD

SPEAK, did the bloud of Abel cry
To God for vengeance ; yes, say I ;
Ev'n as the sprinkled bloud cal'd on
God, for an expiation.

ANOTHER

THE bloud of Abel was a thing
Of such a rev'rend reckoning,
As that the old world thought it fit,
Especially to sweare by it.

A POSITION IN THE HEBREW DIVINITY

ONE man repentant is of more esteem
With God, then one, that never sin'd 'gainst Him.

PENITENCE

THE doctors, in the Talmud, say,
That in this world, one onely day
In true repentance spent, will be
More worth, then heav'ns eternitie.

GODS PRESENCE

GOD's present ev'ry where ; but most of all
Present by union hypostaticall :
God, He is there, where's nothing else, schooles say,
And nothing else is there, where He's away.

THE RESURRECTION POSSIBLE, AND PROBABLE

FOR each one body, that i'th earth is sowne,
There's an up-rising but of one for one :
But for each graine, that in the ground is thrown,
Threescore or fourscore spring up thence for one :
So that the wonder is not halfe so great,
Of ours, as is the rising of the wheat.

CHRISTS SUFFERING

JUSTLY our dearest Saviour may abhorre us,
Who hath more suffer'd by us farre, then for us.

SINNERS

SINNERS confounded are a twofold way,
Either as when (the learned schoolemen say)
Mens sins destroyed are, when they repent ;
Or when, for sins, men suffer punishment.

TEMPTATIONS

No man is tempted so, but may o'recome
If that he has a will to masterdome.

PITTIE, AND PUNISHMENT

God doth embrace the good with love ; & gaines
The good by mercy, as the bad by paines.

GODS PRICE, AND MANS PRICE

God bought man here with his hearts blood expence ;
And man sold God here for base thirty pence.

CHRISTS ACTION

Christ never did so great a work, but there
His humane nature did, in part, appeare :
Or, ne're so meane a peece, but men might see
Therein some beames of His divinitie :
So that, in all He did, there did combine
His humane nature, and His part Divine.

PREDESTINATION

Predestination is the cause alone
Of many standing, but of fall to none.

ANOTHER

Art thou not destin'd ? then, with hast, go on
To make thy faire predestination :
If thou canst change thy life, God then will please
To change, or call back, His past sentences.

SIN

Sin never slew a soule, unlesse there went
Along with it some tempting blandishment.

ANOTHER

Sin is an act so free, that if we shall
Say, 'tis not free, 'tis then no sin at all.

ANOTHER

Sin is the cause of death ; and sin's alone
The cause of Gods predestination :
And from Gods prescience of mans sin doth flow
Our destination to eternall woe.

PRESCIENCE

Gods prescience makes none sinfull ; but th' offence
Of man's the chief cause of God's prescience.

CHRIST

To all our wounds, here, whatsoe're they be,
Christ is the one sufficient remedie.

CHRISTS INCARNATION

Christ took our nature on Him, not that He
'Bove all things lov'd it, for the puritie :
No, but He drest Him with our humane trim,
Because our flesh stood most in need of Him.

HEAVEN

HEAVEN is not given for our good works here :
Yet it is given to the labourer.

GODS KEYES

GOD has foure keyes, which He reserves alone ;
The first of raine, the key of hell next knowne :
With the third key He opes and shuts the wombe ;
And with the fourth key He unlocks the tombe.

SIN

THERE'S no constraint to do amisse,
Whereas but one enforcement is.

ALMES

GIVE unto all, lest he, whom thou deni'st,
May chance to be no other man, but Christ.

HELL-FIRE

ONE onely fire has hell ; but yet it shall,
Not after one sort, there excruciate all :
But look, how each transgressor onward went
Boldly in sin, shall feel more punishment.

TO KEEP A TRUE LENT

Is this a fast, to keep
        The larder leane ?
            And cleane
From fat of veales, and sheep ?

Is it to quit the dish
Of flesh, yet still
To fill
The platter high with fish ?

Is it to fast an houre,
Or rag'd to go,
Or show
A down-cast look, and sowre ?

No : 'tis a fast, to dole
Thy sheaf of wheat,
And meat,
Unto the hungry soule.

It is to fast from strife,
From old debate,
And hate ;
To circumcise thy life.

To shew a heart grief-rent ;
To sterve thy sin,
Not bin ;
And that's to keep thy Lent.

NO TIME IN ETERNITIE

By houres we all live here, in Heaven is known
No spring of Time, or Times succession.

HIS MEDITATION UPON DEATH

Be those few hours, which I have yet to spend,
Blest with the meditation of my end :
Though they be few in number, I'm content ;
If otherwise, I stand indifferent :
Nor makes it matter, Nestors yeers to tell,
If man lives long, and if he live not well.

A multitude of dayes still heaped on,
Seldome brings order, but confusion.
Might I make choice, long life sho'd be withstood;
Nor wo'd I care how short it were, if good:
Which to effect, let ev'ry passing bell
Possesse my thoughts, next comes my dolefull knell:
And when the night perswades me to my bed,
I'le thinke I'm going to be buried:
So shall the blankets which come over me,
Present those turfs, which once must cover me:
And with as firme behaviour I will meet
The sheet I sleep in, as my winding-sheet.
When sleep shall bath his body in mine eyes,
I will believe, that then my body dies:
And if I chance to wake, and rise thereon,
I'le have in mind my resurrection,
Which must produce me to that gen'rall doome,
To which the pesant, so the prince must come,
To heare the Judge give sentence on the throne,
Without the least hope of affection.
Teares, at that day, shall make but weake defence;
When hell and horrour fright the conscience.
Let me, though late, yet at the last, begin
To shun the least temptation to a sin;
Though to be tempted be no sin, untill
Man to th' alluring object gives his will.
Such let my life assure me, when my breath
Goes theeving from me, I am safe in death;
Which is the height of comfort, when I fall,
I rise triumphant in my funerall.

CLOATHS FOR CONTINUANCE

THOSE garments lasting evermore,
Are works of mercy to the poore,
Which neither tettar, time, or moth
Shall fray that silke, or fret this cloth.

TO GOD

COME to me God ; but do not come
To me, as to the gen'rall doome,
In power ; or come Thou in that state,
When Thou Thy lawes didst promulgate,
When as the mountains quak'd for dread,
And sullen clouds bound up his head.
No, lay thy stately terrours by,
To talke with me familiarly ;
For if Thy thunder-claps I heare,
I shall lesse swoone, then die for feare.
Speake Thou of love and I'le reply
By way of epithalamie,
Or sing of mercy, and I'le suit
To it my violl and my lute ;
Thus let Thy lips but love distill,
Then come my God, and hap what will.

THE SOULE

WHEN once the soule has lost her way,
O then, how restlesse do's she stray !
And having not her God for light,
How do's she erre in endlesse night !

THE JUDGMENT-DAY

IN doing justice, God shall then be known,
Who shewing mercy here, few priz'd, or none.

SUFFERINGS

WE merit all we suffer, and by far
More stripes, then God layes on the sufferer.

PAINE AND PLEASURE

GOD suffers not His saints, and servants deere,
To have continuall paine, or pleasure here :
But look how night succeeds the day, so He
Gives them by turnes their grief and jollitie.

GODS PRESENCE

GOD is all-present to what e're we do,
And as all-present, so all-filling too.

ANOTHER

THAT there's a God, we all do know,
But what God is, we cannot show.

THE POORE MANS PART

TELL me rich man, for what intent
Thou load'st with gold thy vestiment ?
When as the poore crie out, to us
Belongs all gold superfluous.

THE RIGHT HAND

GOD has a right hand, but is quite bereft
Of that, which we do nominate the left.

THE STAFFE AND ROD

Two instruments belong unto our God ;
The one a staffe is, and the next a rod :
That if the twig sho'd chance too much to smart,
The staffe might come to play the friendly part.

GOD SPARING IN SCOURGING

God still rewards us more then our desert :
But when He strikes, He quarter-acts His part.

CONFESSION

Confession twofold is, as Austine sayes,
The first of sin is, and the next of praise :
If ill it goes with thee, thy faults confesse :
If well, then chant Gods praise with cheerfulnesse.

GODS DESCENT

God is then said for to descend, when He
Doth, here on earth, some thing of novitie ;
As when, in humane nature He works more
Then ever, yet, the like was done before.

NO COMING TO GOD WITHOUT CHRIST

Good and great God ! how sho'd I feare
To come to Thee, if Christ not there !
Co'd I but think, He would not be
Present, to plead my cause for me ;
To hell I'd rather run, then I
Wo'd see Thy face, and He not by.

ANOTHER, TO GOD

Though Thou beest all that active love,
Which heats those ravisht soules above ;

And though all joyes spring from the glance
Of Thy most winning countenance ;
Yet sowre and grim Thou'dst seem to me ;
If through my Christ I saw not Thee.

THE RESURRECTION

THAT Christ did die, the Pagan saith ;
But that He rose, that's Christians faith.

COHEIRES

WE are coheires with Christ ; nor shall His own
Heire-ship be lesse, by our adoption :
The number here of heires, shall from the state
Of His great birth-right nothing derogate.

THE NUMBER OF TWO

GOD hates the duall number ; being known
The lucklesse number of division :
And when He blest each sev'rall day, whereon
He did His curious operation ;
'Tis never read there, as the fathers say,
God blest His work done on the second day :
Wherefore two prayers ought not to be said,
Or by our selves, or from the pulpit read.

HARDNING OF HEARTS

GOD's said our hearts to harden then,
When as His grace not supples men.

THE ROSE

BEFORE mans fall, the rose was born,
S. Ambrose says, without the thorn :
But, for man's fault, then was the thorn,
Without the fragrant rose-bud, born ;
But ne're the rose without the thorn.

GODS TIME MUST END OUR TROUBLE

GOD doth not promise here to man, that He
Will free him quickly from his miserie ;
But in His own time, and when He thinks fit,
Then He will give a happy end to it.

BAPTISME

THE strength of baptisme, that's within ;
It saves the soule, by drowning sin.

GOLD AND FRANKINCENSE

GOLD serves for tribute to the king ;
The frankincense for Gods offring.

TO GOD

GOD, who me gives a will for to repent ;
Will add a power, to keep me innocent ;
That I shall ne're that trespasse recommit,
When I have done true penance here for it.

THE CHEWING THE CUD

WHEN well we speak, & nothing do that's good,
We not divide the hoof, but chew the cud:
But when good words, by good works, have their proof,
We then both chew the cud, and cleave the hoof.

CHRISTS TWOFOLD COMING

THY former coming was to cure
My soules most desp'rate calenture;
Thy second Advent, that must be
To heale my earths infirmitie.

TO GOD, HIS GIFT

As my little pot doth boyle,
We will keep this levell-coyle;
That a wave, and I will bring
To my God, a heave-offering.

GODS ANGER

GOD can't be wrathfull; but we may conclude,
Wrathfull He may be, by similitude:
God's wrathfull said to be, when He doth do
That without wrath, which wrath doth force us to.

GODS COMMANDS

IN Gods commands, ne're ask the reason why;
Let thy obedience be the best reply.

TO GOD

IF I have plaid the truant, or have here
Fail'd in my part; O! Thou that art my deare,

My mild, my loving tutor, Lord and God !
Correct my errors gently with Thy rod.
I know, that faults will many here be found,
But where sin swells, there let Thy grace abound.

TO GOD

THE work is done ; now let my lawrell be
Given by none, but by Thy selfe, to me :
That done, with honour Thou dost me create
Thy poet, and Thy prophet lawreat.

GOOD FRIDAY : REX TRAGICUS, OR CHRIST GOING TO HIS CROSSE

PUT off Thy robe of purple, then go on
To the sad place of execution :
Thine houre is come ; and the tormentor stands
Ready, to pierce Thy tender feet, and hands.
Long before this, the base, the dull, the rude,
Th' inconstant, and unpurged multitude
Yawne for Thy coming ; some e're this time crie,
How He deferres, how loath He is to die !
Amongst this scumme, the souldier, with his speare,
And that sowre fellow, with his vinegar,
His spunge, and stick, do ask why Thou dost stay ?
So do the skurfe and bran too : Go Thy way,
Thy way, Thou guiltlesse man, and satisfie
By Thine approach, each their beholding eye.
Not as a thief, shalt Thou ascend the mount,
But like a person of some high account :
The crosse shall be Thy stage ; and Thou shalt there
The spacious field have for Thy theater.
Thou art that Roscius, and that markt-out man,
That must this day act the tragedian,
To wonder and affrightment : Thou art He,
Whom all the flux of nations comes to see ;
Not those poor theeves that act their parts with Thee :

Those act without regard, when once a king,
And God, as Thou art, comes to suffering.
No, no, this scene from Thee takes life and sense,
And soule and spirit plot, and excellence.
Why then begin, great King ! ascend Thy throne,
And thence proceed, to act Thy passion
To such an height, to such a period rais'd,
As hell, and earth, and heav'n may stand amaz'd.
God, and good angells guide Thee ; and so blesse
Thee in Thy severall parts of bitternesse ;
That those, who see Thee nail'd unto the tree,
May, though they scorn Thee, praise and pitie Thee.
And we, Thy lovers, while we see Thee keep
The lawes of action, will both sigh, and weep ;
And bring our spices, to embalm Thee dead ;
That done, wee'l see Thee sweetly buried.

HIS WORDS TO CHRIST, GOING TO THE CROSS

When Thou wast taken, Lord, I oft have read,
All Thy disciples Thee forsook, and fled.
Let their example not a pattern be
For me to flie, but now to follow Thee.

ANOTHER, TO HIS SAVIOUR

If Thou beest taken, God forbid,
I flie from Thee, as others did :
But if Thou wilt so honour me,
As to accept my companie,
I'le follow Thee, hap, hap what shall,
Both to the judge, and judgment-hall :
And, if I see Thee posted there,
To be all-flayed with whipping-cheere,
I'le take my share ; or els, my God,
Thy stripes I'le kisse, or burn the rod.

HIS SAVIOURS WORDS, GOING TO THE CROSSE

HAVE, have ye no regard, all ye
Who passe this way, to pitie me,
Who am a man of miserie !

A man both bruis'd, and broke, and one
Who suffers not here for mine own,
But for my friends transgression !

Ah ! Sions daughters, do not feare
The crosse, the cords, the nailes, the speare,
The myrrhe, the gall, the vineger,

For Christ, your loving Saviour, hath
Drunk up the wine of Gods fierce wrath ;
Onely, there's left a little froth,

Lesse for to tast, then for to shew,
What bitter cups had been your due,
Had He not drank them up for you.

HIS ANTHEM, TO CHRIST ON THE CROSSE

WHEN I behold Thee, almost slain,
With one, and all parts, full of pain :
When I Thy gentle heart do see
Pierc't through, and dropping bloud, for me,
I'le call, and cry out, Thanks to Thee.

Vers. But yet it wounds my soule, to think,
That for my sin, Thou, Thou must drink,
Even Thou alone, the bitter cup
Of furie, and of vengeance up.

Chor. Lord, I'le not see Thee to drink all
The vineger, the myrrhe, the gall :

Ver. Chor. But I will sip a little wine ;
Which done, Lord say, *The rest is mine.*

This   cross-tree   here
Doth   JESUS   beare,
Who   sweet'ned   first,
The   death   accurs't.

HERE all things ready are, make hast, make hast away :
For, long this work wil be, & very short this day.
Why then, go on to act : Here's wonders to be done,
Before the last least sand of Thy ninth hour be run ;
Or e're dark clouds do dull, or dead the mid-dayes sun.

Act when Thou wilt,
Bloud will be spilt ;
Pure balm, that shall
Bring health to all.
Why then, begin
To powre first in
Some drops of wine,
In stead of brine,
To search the wound,
So long unsound :
And, when that's done.
Let oyle, next, run,
To cure the sore
Sinne made before.
And O ! deare Christ,
E'en as Thou di'st,
Look down, and see
Us weepe for Thee.
And tho, Love knows,
Thy dreadfull woes
Wee cannot ease ;
Yet doe Thou please,
Who mercie art,
T'accept each heart,
That gladly would
Helpe, if it could.
Meane while, let mee,
Beneath this tree,
This honour have,
To make my grave.

TO HIS SAVIOURS SEPULCHER: HIS DEVOTION

HAILE holy, and all-honour'd tomb,
By no ill haunted ; here I come,
With shoes put off, to tread thy roome.
I'le not prophane, by soile of sin,
Thy doore, as I do enter in :
For I have washt both hand and heart,
This, that, and ev'ry other part ;
So that I dare, with farre lesse feare,
Then full affection, enter here.
Thus, thus I come to kisse Thy stone
With a warm lip, and solemne one :
And as I kisse, I'le here and there
Dresse Thee with flowrie diaper.
How sweet this place is ! as from hence
Flow'd all Panchaia's frankincense ;
Or rich Arabia did commix,
Here, all her rare aromaticks.
Let me live ever here, and stir
No one step from this sepulcher.
Ravisht I am ! and down I lie,
Confus'd, in this brave extasie.
Here let me rest ; and let me have
This for my heaven, that was Thy grave :
And, coveting no higher sphere,
I'le my eternitie spend here.

HIS OFFERING, WITH THE REST, AT THE SEPULCHER

To joyn with them who here confer
Gifts to my Saviours sepulcher ;

Devotion bids me hither bring
Somewhat for my thank-offering.
Loe ! thus I bring a virgin-flower,
To dresse my maiden-Saviour.

HIS COMING TO THE SEPULCHER

HENCE they have born my Lord ; behold ! the stone
Is rowl'd away, and my sweet Saviour's gone.
Tell me, white angell, what is now become
Of Him we lately seal'd up in this tombe ?
Is He, from hence, gone to the shades beneath,
To vanquish hell, as here He conquer'd death ?
If so, I'le thither follow, without feare,
And live in hell, if that my Christ stayes there.

Of all the good things whatsoe're we do,
God is the ΑΡΧΗ, and the ΤΕΛΟΣ too.

HENRY VAUGHAN

DEATH. A DIALOGUE

Soul

'TIS a sad Land, that in one day
Hath dull'd thee thus ; when death shall freeze
Thy blood to ice, and thou must stay
Tenant for years, and centuries ;
How wilt thou brook't ?

Body

I cannot tell ;
But if all sense wings not with thee,
And something still be left the dead,
I'll wish my curtains off, to free
Me from so dark and sad a bed :

A nest of nights, a gloomy sphere,
Where shadows thicken, and the cloud
Sits on the sun's brow all the year,
And nothing moves without a shroud.

Soul

'Tis so : but as thou saw'st that night
We travail'd in, our first attempts
Were dull and blind, but custom straight
Our fears and falls brought to contempt :

Then, when the ghastly twelve was past,
We breath'd still for a blushing East,
And bade the lazy sun make haste,
And on sure hopes, though long, did feast.

But when we saw the clouds to crack,
    And in those crannies light appear'd,
We thought the day then was not slack,
    And pleas'd ourselves with what we fear'd.

Just so it is in death.   But thou
Shalt in thy mother's bosom sleep,
Whilst I each minute groan to know
How near Redemption creeps.

Then shall we meet to mix again, and met,
'Tis last good-night ; our Sun shall never set.

JOB, CAP. 10. VER. 21, 22.

Before I go whence I shall not return, even to the land of darkness and the shadow of death ;
A land of darkness, as darkness itself ; and of the shadow of death, without any order, and where the light is as darkness.

RELIGION

My God, when I walk in those groves
    And leaves, Thy Spirit doth still fan,
I see in each shade that there grows
    An angel talking with a man.

Under a juniper some house,
    Or the cool myrtle's canopy ;
Others beneath an oak's green boughs,
    Or at some fountain's bubbling eye.

Here Jacob dreams, and wrestles ; there
    Elias by a raven is fed ;
Another time by th' angel, where
    He brings him water with his bread.

In Abr'ham's tent the wingèd guests
   —O how familiar then was heaven !—
Eat, drink, discourse, sit down, and rest,
   Until the cool and shady even.

Nay Thou Thyself, my God, in fire,
   Whirlwinds and clouds, and the soft voice,
Speak'st there so much, that I admire
   We have no conf'rence in these days.

Is the truce broke ? or 'cause we have
   A Mediator now with Thee,
Dost Thou therefore old treaties wave,
   And by appeals from Him decree ?

Or is't so, as some green heads say,
   That now all miracles must cease ?
Though Thou hast promis'd they should stay
   The tokens of the Church, and peace.

No, no ; Religion is a spring,
   That from some secret, golden mine
Derives her birth, and thence doth bring
   Cordials in every drop, and wine.

But in her long and hidden course,
   Passing through the Earth's dark veins,
Grows still from better unto worse,
   And both her taste and colour stains ;

Then drilling on, learns to increase
   False echoes and confused sounds,
And unawares doth often seize
   On veins of sulphur under ground ;

So poison'd, breaks forth in some clime,
   And at first sight doth many please ;
But drunk, is puddle, or mere slime,
   And 'stead of physic, a disease.

Just such a tainted sink we have,
    Like that Samaritan's dead well ;
Nor must we for the kernel crave,
    Because most voices like the shell.

Heal then these waters, Lord ; or bring Thy flock,
Since these are troubled, to the springing Rock ;
Look down, Great Master of the feast ; O shine,
And turn once more our water into wine !

CANT. CAP. 4. VER. 12.

My sister, my spouse is as a garden enclosed, as a spring shut up, and a fountain sealed up.

THE RETREAT

HAPPY those early days, when I
Shin'd in my angel-infancy !
Before I understood this place
Appointed for my second race,
Or taught my soul to fancy ought
But a white, celestial thought ;
When yet I had not walk'd above
A mile or two from my first love,
And looking back—at that short space—
Could see a glimpse of His bright face ;
When on some gilded cloud, or flow'r,
My gazing soul would dwell an hour,
And in those weaker glories spy
Some shadows of eternity ;
Before I taught my tongue to wound
My conscience with a sinful sound,
Or had the black art to dispense
A sev'ral sin to ev'ry sense,
But felt through all this fleshly dress
Bright shoots of everlastingness.

O how I long to travel back,
And tread again that ancient track !
That I might once more reach that plain,
Where first I left my glorious train ;
From whence th' enlighten'd spirit sees
That shady City of palm-trees.
But ah ! my soul with too much stay
Is drunk, and staggers in the way !
Some men a forward motion love,
But I by backward steps would move,
And when this dust falls to the urn,
In that state I came, return.

[SURE, THERE'S A TIE OF BODIES ! AND AS THEY]

1

SURE, there's a tie of bodies ! and as they
    Dissolve, with it, to clay,
Love languisheth, and memory doth rust
    O'ercast with that cold dust ;
For things thus centred, without beams or action,
    Nor give nor take contaction ;
And man is such a marigold, these fled,
    That shuts, and hangs the head.

2

Absents within the line conspire, and sense
    Things distant doth unite ;
Herbs sleep unto the East, and some fowls thence
    Watch the returns of light.
But hearts are not so kind : false, short delights
    Tell us the world is brave,

And wrap us in imaginary flights
    Wide of a faithful grave.

3

Thus Lazarus was carried out of town ;
    For 'tis our foes' chief art
By distance all good objects first to drown,
    And then besiege the heart.
But I will be my own death's-head ; and though
    The flatt'rer say, " I live,"
Because incertainties we cannot know,
    Be sure not to believe.

PEACE

My soul, there is a country
    Far beyond the stars,
Where stands a wingèd sentry
    All skilful in the wars :
There, above noise and danger,
    Sweet Peace sits crown'd with smiles,
And One born in a manger
    Commands the beauteous files.
He is thy gracious Friend,
    And—O my soul awake !—
Did in pure love descend,
    To die here for thy sake.
If thou canst get but thither,
    There grows the flower of Peace,
The Rose that cannot wither,
    Thy fortress, and thy ease.
Leave then thy foolish ranges ;
    For none can thee secure,
But One, who never changes,
    Thy God, thy life, thy cure.

THE RELAPSE

My God, how gracious art Thou ! I had slipt
    Almost to hell,
And on the verge of that dark, dreadful pit
    Did hear them yell ;
But O Thy love ! Thy rich, almighty love,
    That sav'd my soul,
And check'd their fury, when I saw them move,
    And heard them howl !
O my sole Comfort, take no more these ways,
    This hideous path,
And I will mend my own without delays :
    Cease Thou Thy wrath !
I have deserv'd a thick, Egyptian damp,
    —Dark as my deeds—
Should mist within me, and put out that lamp
    Thy Spirit feeds ;
A darting conscience full of stabs, and fears ;
    No shade but yew,
Sullen, and sad eclipses, cloudy spheres,
    These are my due.
But He that with His blood—a price too dear—
    My scores did pay,
Bid me, by virtue from Him, challenge here
    The brightest day ;
Sweet, downy thoughts, soft lily-shades, calm streams,
    Joys full, and true,
Fresh, spicy mornings, and eternal beams,—
    These are His due.

CORRUPTION

Sure, it was so. Man in those early days
    Was not all stone and earth ;
He shin'd a little, and by those weak rays
    Had some glimpse of his birth.

He saw heaven o'er his head, and knew from whence
    He came, condemnèd, hither ;
And, as first love draws strongest, so from hence
    His mind sure progress'd thither.

Things here were strange unto him ; sweat and till ;
    All was a thorn or weed ;
Nor did those last, but—like himself—died still
    As soon as they did seed ;

They seem'd to quarrel with him ; for that act,
    That fell him, foil'd them all ;
He drew the curse upon the world, and crack'd
    The whole frame with his fall.

This made him long for home, as loth to stay
    With murmurers and foes ;
He sigh'd for Eden, and would often say
    " Ah ! what bright days were those ! "

Nor was heav'n cold unto him ; for each day
    The valley or the mountain
Afforded visits, and still Paradise lay
    In some green shade or fountain.

Angels lay leiger here ; each bush, and cell,
    Each oak, and highway knew them ;
Walk but the fields, or sit down at some well,
    And he was sure to view them.

Almighty Love ! where art Thou now ? mad man
    Sits down and freezeth on ;
He raves, and swears to stir nor fire, nor fan,
    But bids the thread be spun.

I see, Thy curtains are close-drawn ; Thy bow
    Looks dim too in the cloud ;
Sin triumphs still, and man is sunk below
    The centre, and his shroud.

All's in deep sleep and night : thick darkness lies
    And hatcheth o'er Thy people—
But hark ! what trumpet's that ? what angel cries
    " Arise ! thrust in Thy sickle ? "

CHRIST'S NATIVITY

I

AWAKE, glad heart ! get up, and sing !
It is the birthday of thy King.
    Awake ! awake !
    The sun doth shake
Light from his locks, and all the way
Breathing perfumes, doth spice the day.

Awake, awake ! hark how th' wood rings,
Winds whisper, and the busy springs
    A consort make ;
    Awake ! awake !
Man is their high-priest, and should rise
To offer up the sacrifice.

I would I were some bird, or star,
Flutt'ring in woods, or lifted far
    Above this inn
    And road of sin !
Then either star, or bird, should be
Shining, or singing still, to Thee.

I would I had in my best part
Fit rooms for Thee ! or that my heart
    Were so clean as
    Thy manger was !
But I am all filth, and obscene ;
Yet if Thou wilt, Thou canst make clean.

Sweet Jesu ! will then ; let no more
This leper haunt, and soil Thy door !
    Cure him, ease him,
    O release him !

And let once more, by mystic birth,
The Lord of life be borne in Earth.

II

How kind is Heav'n to man !   If here
    One sinner doth amend,
Straight there is joy, and ev'ry sphere
    In music doth contend ;
And shall we then no voices lift ?
    Are mercy, and salvation
Not worth our thanks ?   Is life a gift
    Of no more acceptation ?
Shall He that did come down from thence,
    And here for us was slain,
Shall He be now cast off ? no sense
    Of all His woes remain ?
Can neither love, nor suff'rings bind ?
    Are we all stone, and earth ?
Neither His bloody passions mind,
    Nor one day bless His birth ?
Alas, my God !   Thy birth now here
Must not be number'd in the year.

IDLE VERSE

Go, go, quaint follies, sugar'd sin,
    Shadow no more my door !
I will no longer cobwebs spin ;
    I'm too much on the score.

For since amidst my youth and night
    My great Preserver smiles,
We'll make a match, my only light,
    And join against their wiles :

Blind, desp'rate fits, that study how
    To dress, and trim our shame ;
That gild rank poison, and allow
    Vice in a fairer name ;

The purls of youthful blood, and bowls,
    Lust in the robes of Love,
The idle talk of fev'rish souls
    Sick with a scarf, or glove ;

Let it suffice, my warmer days
    Simper'd and shin'd on you ;
Twist not my cypress with your bays,
    Or roses with my yew.

Go, go, seek out some greener thing,
    It snows and freezeth here ;
Let nightingales attend the Spring,
    Winter is all my year.

SON—DAYS

I

BRIGHT shadows of true rest ! some shoots of bliss :
    Heaven once a week ;
The next world's gladness prepossess'd in this ;
    A day to seek
Eternity in time ; the steps by which
  We climb above all ages ; lamps that light
Man through his heap of dark days ; and the rich
  And full redemption of the whole week's flight !

2

The pulleys unto headlong man ; Time's bower ;
    The narrow way ;

Transplanted Paradise ; God's walking hour,
          The cool o' th' day !
The creature's jubilee ; God's parle with dust ;
     Heaven here ; man on those hills of myrrh, and
          flowers :
Angels descending ; the returns of trust ;
     A gleam of glory after six-days-showers !

3

The Church's love-feasts ; Time's prerogative,
          And interest
Deducted from the whole ; the combs, and hive,
          And home of rest.
The milky way chalk'd out with suns ; a clue
     That guides through erring hours ; and in full story
A taste of heav'n on earth ; the pledge and cue
     Of a full feast ; and the out-Courts of glory.

THE BURIAL OF AN INFANT

BLEST infant bud, whose blossom-life
     Did only look about, and fall,
Wearied out in a harmless strife
     Of tears and milk, the food of all !

Sweetly didst thou expire : thy soul
     Flew home unstain'd by his new kin ;
For ere thou knew'st how to be foul,
     Death wean'd thee from the world, and sin.

Softly rest all thy virgin-crumbs !
     Lapp'd in the sweets of thy young breath,
Expecting till thy Saviour comes
     To dress them, and unswaddle death.

THE DAWNING ✗

AH ! what time wilt Thou come ? when shall that cry
" The Bridegroom's coming ! " fill the sky ?
Shall it in the evening run
When our words and works are done ?
Or will Thy all-surprising light
      Break at midnight,
When either sleep, or some dark pleasure
Possesseth mad man without measure ?
Or shall these early, fragrant hours
      Unlock Thy bowers ?
And with their blush of light descry
Thy locks crown'd with eternity ?
Indeed, it is the only time
That with Thy glory doth best chime ;
All now are stirring, ev'ry field
      Full hymns doth yield ;
The whole creation shakes off night,
And for Thy shadow looks, the light ;
Stars now vanish without number,
Sleepy planets set and slumber,
The pursy clouds disband and scatter,
All expect some sudden matter,
Not one beam triumphs, but from far
      That morning-star.
O at what time soever Thou,
Unknown to us, the heavens wilt bow,
And with Thy angels in the van,
Descend to judge poor careless man,
Grant I may not like puddle lie
In a corrupt security.
Where, if a traveller water crave,
He finds it dead, and in a grave ;
But at this restless, vocal spring
All day and night doth run and sing,

And though here born, yet is acquainted
Elsewhere, and flowing keeps untainted ;
So let me all my busy age
In Thy free services engage ;
And though—while here—of force I must
Have commerce sometimes with poor dust,
And in my flesh, though vile and low,
As this doth in her channel flow,
You let my course, my aim, my love,
And chief acquaintance be above ;
So when that day and hour shall come,
In which Thy Self will be the sun,
Thou'lt find me dress'd and on my way,
Watching the break of Thy great day.

THE PILGRIMAGE

As travellers, when the twilight's come,
   And in the sky the stars appear,
The past day's accidents do sum
   With " Thus we saw there, and thus here ; "

Then Jacob-like lodge in a place,
   —A place, and no more, is set down—
Where till the day restore the race,
   They rest and dream homes of their own :

So for this night I linger here,
   And full of tossings to and fro,
Expect still when Thou wilt appear,
   That I may get me up and go.

I long, and groan, and grieve for Thee,
   For Thee my words, my tears do gush ;
O that I were but where I see !
   Is all the note within my bush.

As birds robb'd of their native wood,
  Although their diet may be fine,
Yet neither sing, nor like their food,
  But with the thought of home do pine ;

So do I mourn, and hang my head ;
  And though Thou dost me fulness give,
Yet look I for far better bread,
  Because by this man cannot live.

O feed me then ! and since I may
  Have yet more days, more nights to count,
So strengthen me, Lord, all the way,
  That I may travel to Thy mount.

HEB. CAP. XI. VER. 13.

*And they confessed that they were strangers and pilgrims
on the earth.*

THE WORLD

I

I SAW Eternity the other night,
Like a great ring of pure and endless light,
    All calm, as it was bright ;
And round beneath it, Time in hours, days, years,
        Driv'n by the spheres
Like a vast shadow mov'd ; in which the world
        And all her train were hurl'd.
The doting lover in his quaintest strain
        Did there complain ;
Near him, his lute, his fancy, and his flights,
        Wit's sour delights ;
With gloves, and knots, the silly snares of pleasure,
        Yet his dear treasure,
All scatter'd lay, while he his eyes did pour
        Upon a flow'r.

2

The darksome statesman, hung with weights and woe,
Like a thick midnight-fog, mov'd there so slow,
      He did nor stay, nor go ;
Condemning thoughts—like sad eclipses—scowl
         Upon his soul,
And clouds of crying witnesses without
       Pursued him with one shout.
Yet digg'd the mole, and lest his ways be found,
       Work'd under ground,
Where he did clutch his prey ; but one did see
       That policy :
Churches and altars fed him ; perjuries
       Were gnats and flies ;
It rain'd about him blood and tears, but he
       Drank them as free.

3

The fearful miser on a heap of rust
Sate pining all his life there, did scarce trust
      His own hands with the dust,
Yet would not place one piece above, but lives
      In fear of thieves.
Thousands there were as frantic as himself,
      And hugg'd each one his pelf ;
The downright epicure plac'd heav'n in sense,
      And scorn'd pretence ;
While others, slipp'd into a wide excess,
      Said little less ;
The weaker sort slight, trivial wares enslave,
      Who think them brave ;
And poor, despisèd Truth sate counting by
      Their victory.

4

Yet some, who all this while did weep and sing,
And sing, and weep, soar'd up into the ring ;
   But most would use no wing.
O fools—said I—thus to prefer dark night
   Before true light !
To live in grots and caves, and hate the day
   Because it shows the way ;
The way, which from this dead and dark abode
   Leads up to God ;
A way where you might tread the sun, and be
   More bright than he !
But as I did their madness so discuss,
   One whisper'd thus,
" This ring the Bridegroom did for none provide,
   But for His bride."

JOHN, CAP. 2. VER. 16, 17.

*All that is in the world, the lust of the flesh, the lust of
the eyes, and the pride of life, is not of the Father, but is
of the world.*

*And the world passeth away, and the lusts thereof ; but
he that doeth the will of God abideth for ever.*

MAN

I

WEIGHING the steadfastness and state
Of some mean things which here below reside,
Where birds, like watchful clocks, the noiseless date
   And intercourse of times divide,
Where bees at night get home and hive, and flow'rs
   Early as well as late,
Rise with the sun and set in the same bow'rs ;

2

I would—said I—my God would give
The staidness of these things to man ! for these
To His divine appointments ever cleave,
    And no new business breaks their peace ;
The birds nor sow nor reap, yet sup and dine ;
       The flow'rs without clothes live,
Yet Solomon was never dress'd so fine.

3

Man hath still either toys, or care ;
He hath no root, nor to one place is tied,
But ever restless and irregular
    About this Earth doth run and ride.
He knows he hath a home, but scarce knows where ;
       He says it is so far,
That he hath quite forgot how to go there.

4

He knocks at all doors, strays and roams,
Nay, hath not so much wit as some stones have,
Which in the darkest nights point to their homes,
    By some hid sense their Maker gave ;
Man is the shuttle, to whose winding quest
       And passage through these looms
God order'd motion, but ordain'd no rest.

ASCENSION-DAY

LORD JESUS ! with what sweetness and delights,
Sure, holy hopes, high joys, and quick'ning flights,
Dost Thou feed Thine ! O Thou ! the Hand that lifts
To Him, Who gives all good and perfect gifts,
Thy glorious, bright Ascension—though remov'd

So many ages from me—is so prov'd
And by Thy Spirit seal'd to me, that I
Feel me a sharer in Thy victory.

　　　　I soar and rise
　　　　Up to the skies,
　　　　　Leaving the world their day,
　　　　And in my flight
　　　　For the true light
　　　　　Go seeking all the way.

I greet Thy sepulchre, salute Thy grave,
That blest enclosure, where the angels gave
The first glad tidings of Thy early light,
And resurrection from the earth and night.
I see that morning in Thy convert's tears,
Fresh as the dew, which but this dawning wears.
I smell her spices ; and her ointment yields
As rich a scent as the now primros'd fields :
The Day-star smiles, and light, with Thee deceas'd,
Now shines in all the chambers of the East.
What stirs, what posting intercourse and mirth
Of saints and angels glorify the Earth !
What sighs, what whispers, busy stops and stays ;
Private and holy talk fill all the ways !
They pass as at the last great day, and run
In their white robes to seek the Risen Sun ;
I see them, hear them, mark their haste, and move
Amongst them, with them, wing'd with faith and love.
Thy forty days more secret commerce here,
After Thy death and funeral, so clear
And indisputable shows to my sight
As the sun doth, which to those days gave light.
I walk the fields of Bethany, which shine
All now as fresh as Eden, and as fine.
Such was the bright world, on the first seventh day,
Before man brought forth sin, and sin decay ;
When like a virgin, clad in flowers and green,
The pure Earth sat ; and the fair woods had seen
No frost, but flourish'd in that youthful vest,

With which their great Creator had them dress'd ;
When heav'n above them shin'd like molten glass,
　　While all the planets did unclouded pass ;
And springs, like dissolv'd pearls, their streams did pour,
Ne'er marr'd with floods, nor anger'd with a show'r.
With these fair thoughts I move in this fair place,
　　And the last steps of my mild Master trace ;
I see Him leading out His chosen train
　　All sad with tears ; which like warm Summer rain
In silent drops steal from their holy eyes,
　　Fix'd lately on the Cross, now on the skies.
And now, eternal Jesus, Thou dost heave
　　Thy blessed hands to bless these Thou dost leave ;
The Cloud doth now receive Thee, and their sight
　　Having lost Thee, behold two men in white !
Two and no more : " What two attest, is true,
　　Was Thine own answer to the stubborn Jew.
Come then, Thou faithful Witness ! come, dear Lord,
Upon the clouds again to judge this world !

[THEY ARE ALL GONE INTO THE WORLD
OF LIGHT]

THEY are all gone into the world of light !
　　　　And I alone sit ling'ring here ;
Their very memory is fair and bright,
　　　　And my sad thoughts doth clear.

It glows and glitters in my cloudy breast,
　　　　Like stars upon some gloomy grove,
Or those faint beams in which this hill is dress'd,
　　　　After the sun's remove.

I see them walking in an air of glory,
　　　　Whose light doth trample on my days :
My days, which are at best but dull and hoary,
　　　　Mere glimmering and decays.

O holy Hope ! and high Humility,
    High as the heavens above !
These are your walks, and you have show'd them me,
    To kindle my cold love.

Dear, beauteous Death ! the jewel of the just,
    Shining nowhere, but in the dark ;
What mysteries do lie beyond thy dust,
    Could man outlook that mark !

He that hath found some fledg'd bird's nest, may know
    At first sight, if the bird be flown ;
But what fair well or grove he sings in now,
    That is to him unknown.

And yet, as angels in some brighter dreams
    Call to the soul when man doth sleep,
So some strange thoughts transcend our wonted themes,
    And into glory peep.

If a star were confin'd into a tomb,
    Her captive flames must needs burn there ;
But when the hand that lock'd her up, gives room,
    She'll shine through all the sphere.

O Father of eternal life, and all
    Created glories under Thee !
Resume Thy spirit from this world of thrall
    Into true liberty.

Either disperse these mists, which blot and fill
    My perspective still as they pass :
Or else remove me hence unto that hill
    Where I shall need no glass.

PALM-SUNDAY

Come, drop your branches, strew the way,
        Plants of the day !
Whom sufferings make most green and gay.
The King of grief, the Man of Sorrow,
Weeping still, like the wet morrow,
Your shades and freshness comes to borrow.

Put on, put on your best array ;
Let the joy'd road make holiday,
And flowers, that into fields do stray
Or secret groves, keep the highway.

Trees, flowers, and herbs ; birds, beasts, and stones,
That since man fell, expect with groans
To see the Lamb, which [?] all at once,
Lift up your heads, and leave your moans ;
        For here comes He
        Whose death will be
Man's life, and your full liberty.

Hark ! how the children shrill and high
        " Hosanna " cry ;
Their joys provoke the distant sky,
Where thrones and seraphins reply ;

And their own angels shine and sing,
        In a bright ring :
        Such young, sweet mirth
        Makes heaven and earth
Join in a joyful symphony.

The harmless, young, and happy ass,
—Seen long before this came to pass—
Is in these joys an high partaker,
Ordain'd and made to bear his Maker.

Dear feast of palms, of flowers and dew !
  Whose fruitful dawn sheds hopes and lights ;
Thy bright solemnities did shew
  The third glad day through two sad nights.

I'll get me up before the sun,
  I'll cut me boughs off many a tree,
And all alone full early run
  To gather flowers to welcome Thee.

Then like the palm, though wrong'd I'll bear,
  I will be still a child, still meek
As the poor ass, which the proud jeer,
  And only my dear Jesus seek.

If I lose all, and must endure
  The proverb'd griefs of holy Job,
I care not, so I may secure
  But one green branch and a white robe.

THE KNOT

BRIGHT Queen of Heaven ! God's Virgin Spouse !
    The glad world's blessed Maid !
Whose beauty tied life to thy house,
    And brought us saving aid.

Thou art the true Love's-knot ; by thee
    God is made our ally ;
And man's inferior essence He
    With His did dignify.

For coalescent by that band
    We are His body grown,
Nourish'd with favours from His hand
    Whom for our Head we own.

And such a knot, what arm dares loose,
      What life, what death can sever?
Which us in Him, and Him in us,
      United keeps for ever.

AS TIME ONE DAY BY ME DID PASS

As Time one day by me did pass,
      Through a large dusky glass
      He held, I chanc'd to look,
      And spied his curious book
Of past days, where sad Heav'n did shed
A mourning light upon the dead.

Many disorder'd lives I saw,
      And foul records, which thaw
      My kind eyes still, but in
      A fair, white page of thin
And ev'n, smooth lines, like the sun's rays,
Thy name was writ, and all thy days.

O bright and happy kalendar!
      Where youth shines like a star
      All pearl'd with tears, and may
      Teach age the holy way;
Where through thick pangs, high agonies,
Faith into life breaks, and Death dies.

As some meek night-piece which day quails,
      To candle-light unveils:
      So by one beamy line
      From thy bright lamp, did shine
In the same page thy humble grave,
Set with green herbs, glad hopes and brave.

Here slept my thought's dear mark! which dust
      Seem'd to devour, like rust;

But dust—I did observe—
 By hiding doth preserve ;
As we for long and sure recruits,
Candy with sugar our choice fruits.

O calm and sacred bed, where lies
 In death's dark mysteries
 A beauty far more bright
 Than the noon's cloudless light ;
For whose dry dust green branches bud,
And robes are bleach'd in the Lamb's blood.

Sleep, happy ashes !—blessed sleep !—
 While hapless I still weep ;
 Weep that I have outliv'd
 My life, and unreliev'd
Must—soulless shadow !—so live on,
Though life be dead, and my joys gone.

THE DWELLING-PLACE

St. John, Cap. i. ver. 38, 39.

What happy, secret fountain,
Fair shade, or mountain,
Whose undiscover'd virgin glory
Boasts it this day, though not in story,
Was then Thy dwelling ? did some cloud,
Fix'd to a tent, descend and shroud
My distress'd Lord ? or did a star,
Beckon'd by Thee, though high and far,
In sparkling smiles haste gladly down
To lodge light, and increase her own ?
My dear, dear God ! I do not know
What lodg'd Thee then, nor where, nor how ;
But I am sure Thou dost now come
Oft to a narrow, homely room,
Where Thou too hast but the least part ;
My God, I mean my sinful heart.

CHILDHOOD

I CANNOT reach it ; and my striving eye
Dazzles at it, as at eternity.

        Were now that chronicle alive,
Those white designs which children drive,
And the thoughts of each harmless hour,
With their content too in my pow'r,
Quickly would I make my path ev'n,
And by mere playing go to heaven.

        Why should men love
A wolf, more than a lamb or dove ?
Or choose hell-fire and brimstone streams
Before bright stars and God's own beams ?
Who kisseth thorns will hurt his face,
But flowers do both refresh and grace ;
And sweetly living—fie on men !—
Are, when dead, medicinal then ;
If seeing much should make staid eyes,
And long experience should make wise ;
Since all that age doth teach is ill,
Why should I not love childhood still ?
Why, if I see a rock or shelf,
Shall I from thence cast down myself ?
Or by complying with the world,
From the same precipice be hurl'd ?
Those observations are but foul,
Which make me wise to lose my soul.

And yet the practice worldlings call
Business, and weighty action all,
Checking the poor child for his play,
But gravely cast themselves away.

Dear, harmless age ! the short, swift span
Where weeping Virtue parts with man ;
Where love without lust dwells, and bends
What way we please without self-ends.

An age of mysteries ! which he
Must live twice that would God's face see
Which angels guard, and with it play,
Angels ! which foul men drive away.

How do I study now, and scan
Thee more than e'er I studied man,
And only see through a long night
Thy edges and thy bordering light !
O for thy centre and midday !
For sure that is the narrow way !

THE NIGHT

John, Cap. 3. ver. 2.

Through that pure virgin shrine,
That sacred veil drawn o'er Thy glorious noon,
That men might look and live, as glow-worms shine,
And face the moon :
Wise Nicodemus saw such light
As made him know his God by night.

Most blest believer he !
Who in that land of darkness and blind eyes
Thy long-expected healing wings could see
When Thou didst rise !
And, what can never more be done,
Did at midnight speak with the Sun !

O who will tell me, where
He found Thee at that dead and silent hour ?
What hallow'd solitary ground did bear
    So rare a flower ;
      Within whose sacred leaves did lie
      The fulness of the Deity ?

    No mercy-seat of gold,
No dead and dusty cherub, nor carv'd stone,
But His own living works did my Lord hold
    And lodge alone ;
      Where trees and herbs did watch and peep
      And wonder, while the Jews did sleep.

    Dear Night ! this world's defeat ;
The stop to busy fools ; care's check and curb ;
The day of spirits ; my soul's calm retreat
    Which none disturb !
      Christ's progress, and His prayer-time ,
      The hours to which high Heaven doth chime.

    God's silent, searching flight ;
When my Lord's head is fill'd with dew, and all
His locks are wet with the clear drops of night ;
    His still, soft call ;
      His knocking-time ; the soul's dumb watch,
      When spirits their fair kindred catch.

    Were all my loud, evil days
Calm and unhaunted as is thy dark tent,
Whose peace but by some angel's wing or voice
    Is seldom rent ;
      Then I in heaven all the long year
      Would keep, and never wander here.

    But living where the sun
Doth all things wake, and where all mix and tire

Themselves and others, I consent and run
        To ev'ry mire :
    And by this world's ill-guiding light,
    Err more than I can do by night.

    There is in God—some say—
A deep, but dazzling darkness ; as men here
Say it is late and dusky, because they
        See not all clear.
    O for that Night ! where I in Him
    Might live invisible and dim !

THE AGREEMENT

I WROTE it down.   But one that saw
    And envied that record, did since
Such a mist over my mind draw,
    It quite forgot that purpos'd glimpse,
        I read it sadly oft, but still
        Simply believ'd 'twas not my quill.

At length my life's kind angel came,
    And with his bright and busy wing
Scatt'ring that cloud show'd me the flame,
    Which straight like morning-stars did sing
        And shine, and point me to a place,
        Which all the year sees the sun's face.

O beamy book ! O my midday,
    Exterminating fears and night !
The mount, whose white ascendants may
    Be in conjunction with true light !
        My thoughts, when towards Thee they move,
        Glitter and kindle with Thy love.

Thou art the oil and the wine-house ;
    Thine are the present healing leaves,

Blown from the tree of life to us
  By His breath whom my dead heart heaves.
  Each page of Thine hath true life in't,
    And God's bright mind express'd in print.

Most modern books are blots on Thee,
  Their doctrine chaff and windy fits,
Darken'd along, as their scribes be,
  With those foul storms, when they were writ;
    While the man's zeal lays out and blends
    Only self-worship and self-ends.

Thou art the faithful, pearly rock,
  The hive of beamy, living lights,
Ever the same, whose diffus'd stock
  Entire still wears out blackest nights.
    Thy lines are rays the true Sun sheds;
    Thy leaves are healing wings He spreads.

For until Thou didst comfort me
  I had not one poor word to say:
Thick busy clouds did multiply,
  And said, I was no child of day;
    They said, my own hands did remove
    That candle given me from above.

O God! I know and do confess
  My sins are great and still prevail:
Most heinous sins and numberless!
  But Thy compassions cannot fail.
    If Thy sure mercies can be broken,
    Then all is true my foes have spoken.

But while Time runs, and after it
  Eternity, which never ends,
Quite through them both, still infinite,
  Thy covenant by Christ extends;
    No sins of frailty, nor of youth,
    Can foil His merits, and Thy truth.

And this I hourly find, for Thou
  Dost still renew, and purge and heal
Thy care and love, which jointly flow,
  New cordials, new cathartics deal.
    But were I once cast off by Thee,
    I know—my God !—this would not be.

Wherefore with tears—tears by Thee sent—
  I beg my faith may never fail !
And when in death my speech is spent,
  O let that silence then prevail !
    O chase in that cold calm my foes,
    And hear my heart's last private throes !

So Thou Who didst the work begin
  —For I till drawn came not to Thee—
Wilt finish it, and by no sin
  Will Thy free mercies hind'red be.
    For which, O God, I only can
    Bless Thee, and blame unthankful man.

THE DAY OF JUDGMENT

O DAY of life, of light, of love !
The only day dealt from above !
A day so fresh, so bright, so brave,
'Twill show us each forgotten grave,
And make the dead, like flowers, arise
Youthful and fair to see new skies.
All other days, compared to thee,
Are but Light's weak minority ;
They are but veils, and cypress drawn
Like clouds, before thy glorious dawn.
O come ! arise ! shine ! do not stay,
      Dearly lov'd day !
The fields are long since white, and I
With earnest groans for freedom cry ;

My fellow-creatures too say " Come ! "
And stones, though speechless, are not dumb.
When shall we hear that glorious voice
  Of life and joys ?
That voice, which to each secret bed
  Of my Lord's dead,
Shall bring true day, and make dust see
The way to immortality ?
When shall those first white pilgrims rise,
Whose holy, happy histories
—Because they sleep so long—some men
Count but the blots of a vain pen ?
  Dear Lord ! make haste !
Sin every day commits more waste ;
And Thy old enemy, which knows
His time is short, more raging grows.
Nor moan I only—though profuse—
Thy creature's bondage and abuse ;
But what is highest sin and shame,
The vile despite done to Thy name ;
The forgeries, which impious wit
And power force on Holy Writ,
With all detestable designs,
That may dishonour those pure lines.
O God ! though mercy be in Thee
The greatest attribute we see,
And the most needful for our sins ;
Yet, when Thy mercy nothing wins
But mere disdain, let not man say
" Thy arm doth sleep," but write this day
Thy judging one : descend, descend !
Make all things new, and without end !

THE WATERFALL

WITH what deep murmurs, through Time's silent stealth,
Doth thy transparent, cool, and wat'ry wealth,

Here flowing fall,
And chide and call,
As if his liquid, loose retinue stay'd
Ling'ring, and were of this steep place afraid,
The common pass,
Where clear as glass,
All must descend
Not to an end,
But quick'ned by this deep and rocky grave,
Rise to a longer course more bright and brave.

Dear stream ! dear bank ! where often I
Have sat, and pleased my pensive eye ;
Why, since each drop of thy quick store
Runs thither whence it flow'd before,
Should poor souls fear a shade or night,
Who came—sure—from a sea of light ?
Or, since those drops are all sent back
So sure to Thee that none doth lack,
Why should frail flesh doubt any more
That what God takes He'll not restore ?
O useful element and clear !
My sacred wash and cleanser here ;
My first consigner unto those
Fountains of life, where the Lamb goes !
What sublime truths and wholesome themes
Lodge in thy mystical, deep streams !
Such as dull man can never find,
Unless that Spirit lead his mind,
Which first upon thy face did move
And hatch'd all with His quick'ning love.
As this loud brook's incessant fall
In streaming rings restagnates all,
Which reach by course the bank, and then
Are no more seen : just so pass men.
O my invisible estate,
My glorious liberty, still late !

Thou art the channel my soul seeks,
Not this with cataracts and creeks.

QUICKNESS

FALSE life ! a foil and no more, when
     Wilt thou be gone ?
Thou foul deception of all men,
That would not have the true come on !

Thou art a moon-like toil ; a blind
     Self-posing state ;
A dark contest of waves and wind ;
A mere tempestuous debate.

Life is a fix'd, discerning light,
     A knowing joy ;
No chance, or fit ; but ever bright,
And calm, and full, yet doth not cloy.

'Tis such a blissful thing, that still
     Doth vivify,
And shine and smile, and hath the skill
To please without eternity.

Thou art a toilsome mole, or less,
     A moving mist.
But life is, what none can express,
A quickness, which my God hath kiss'd.

TO THE HOLY BIBLE

O BOOK ! Life's guide ! how shall we part ;
And thou so long seiz'd of my heart ?
Take this last kiss ; and let me weep
True thanks to thee before I sleep.

Thou wert the first put in my hand,
When yet I could not understand,
And daily didst my young eyes lead
To letters, till I learnt to read.
But as rash youths, when once grown strong,
Fly from their nurses to the throng,
Where they new consorts choose, and stick
To those till either hurt or sick ;
So with that first light gain'd from thee
Ran I in chase of vanity,
Cried dross for gold, and never thought
My first cheap book had all I sought.
Long reign'd this vogue ; and thou cast by,
With meek, dumb looks didst woo mine eye,
And oft left open, wouldst convey
A sudden and most searching ray
Into my soul, with whose quick touch
Refining still I struggled much.
By this mild art of love at length
Thou overcam'st my sinful strength,
And having brought me home, didst there
Show me that pearl I sought elsewhere,
Gladness, and peace, and hope, and love,
The secret favours of the Dove ;
Her quick'ning kindness, smiles and kisses,
Exalted pleasures, crowning blisses,
Fruition, union, glory, life,
Thou didst lead to, and still all strife.
Living, thou wert my soul's sure ease,
And dying mak'st me go in peace :
Thy next effects no tongue can tell ;
Farewell, O book of God ! farewell !

ST. LUKE, CAP. 2. VER. 14.

Glory to God in the highest, and on earth peace, good will towards men.

THOMAS TRAHERNE

THE SALUTATION

THESE little Limbs,
These Eys & Hands wch here I find,
This panting Heart wherwith my Life begins ;
Where have ye been ? Behind
What Curtain were ye from me hid so long !
Where was, in what Abyss, my new-made Tongue ?

When silent I
So many thousand thousand Years
Beneath the Dust did in a *Chaos* ly,
How could I *Smiles*, or *Tears*,
Or *Lips*, or *Hands*, or *Eys*, or *Ears* perceiv ?
Welcom ye Treasures wch I now receiv.

I that so long
Was *Nothing* from Eternity,
Did little think such Joys as Ear & Tongue
To celebrat or see :
Such Sounds to hear, such Hands to feel, such Feet,
Such Eys & Objects, on the Ground to meet.

New burnisht Joys !
Which finest Gold & Pearl excell !
Such sacred Treasures are the Limbs of Boys
In which a Soul doth dwell :
Their organized Joints & azure Veins
More Wealth include than the dead World conteins.

From Dust I rise
And out of Nothing now awake ;

These brighter Regions wch salute mine Eys
　　A Gift from God I take :
The Earth, the Seas, the Light, the lofty Skies,
The Sun & Stars are mine ; if these I prize.

　　A Stranger here
　Strange things doth meet, strange Glory see,
Strange Treasures lodg'd in this fair World appear,
　　Strange all & New to me :
But that they *mine* should be who Nothing was,
That Strangest is of all ; yet brought to pass.

WONDER

　How like an Angel came I down !
　　How bright are all things here !
When first among his Works I did appear
　　O how their Glory did me crown !
The World resembled his ETERNITY,
　　In which my Soul did walk ;
　　And evry thing that I did see
　　　Did with me talk.

　The Skies in their Magnificence,
　　The lovly lively Air,
Oh how divine, how soft, how sweet, how fair !
　　The Stars did entertain my Sense ;
And all the Works of God so bright & pure,
　　So rich & great, did seem,
　　As if they ever must endure
　　　In my Esteem.

　A Nativ Health & Innocence
　　Within my Bones did grow,
And while my God did all his Glories show
　　I felt a vigor in my Sense

That was all SPIRIT : I within did flow
        With Seas of Life like Wine ;
I nothing in the World did know
        But 'twas Divine.

Harsh rugged Objects were conceal'd,
        Oppressions, Tears, & Cries,
Sins, Griefs, Complaints, Dissentions, weeping Eys,
        Were hid : And only things reveal'd
Which hevenly Spirits & the Angels prize :
        The State of Innocence
        And Bliss, not Trades & Poverties,
                Did fill my Sense.

The Streets seem'd paved wth golden Stones,
        The Boys & Girls all mine ;
To me how did their lovly faces shine !
        The Sons of men all Holy ones,
In Joy & Beauty, then appear'd to me ;
        And evry Thing I found
        (While like an Angel I did see)
                Adorn'd the Ground.

Rich Diamonds, & Pearl, & Gold
        Might evry where be seen ;
Rare Colors, yellow, blew, red, white, & green
        Mine Eys on evry side behold :
All that I saw, a Wonder did appear,
        Amazement was my Bliss :
        That & my Wealth met evry where.
                No Joy to this !

Curs'd, ill-devis'd Proprieties
        With Envy, Avarice,
And Fraud, (those Fiends that spoil ev'n Paradise)
        Were not the Object of mine Eys ;

Nor Hedges, Ditches, Limits, narrow Bounds :
    I dreamt not ought of those,
  But in surveying all mens Grounds
    I found Repose.

For Property its self was mine,
    And Hedges, Ornaments :
Walls, Houses, Coffers, & their rich Contents,
    To make me Rich combine.
Cloaths, costly Jewels, Laces, I esteem'd
    My Wealth by others worn,
For me they all to wear them seem'd,
    When I was born.

THE PRÆPARATIVE

My Body being dead, my Limbs unknown ;
    Before I skill'd to prize
    Those living Stars, mine Eys ;
Before or Tongue or Cheeks I call'd mine own,
  Before I knew these Hands were mine,
Or that my Sinews did my Members join ;
    When neither Nostril, foot, nor Ear,
As yet could be discern'd, or did appear ;
    I was within
A House I knew not, newly cloath'd wth Skin.

Then was my Soul my only All to me,
    A living endless Ey,
    Scarce bounded with the Sky,
Whose Power, & Act, & Essence was to see :
    I was an inward Sphere of Light,
Or an interminable Orb of Sight,
    Exceeding that wch makes the Days,
A *vital* Sun that shed abroad his Rays :
    All Life, all Sense,
A naked, simple, pure Intelligence.

I then no Thirst nor Hunger did perceiv ;
      No dire Necessity
      Nor Want was known to me :
Without disturbance then I did receiv
    The tru Ideas of all Things,
The Hony did enjoy without the Stings.
    A meditating inward Ey
Gazing at Quiet did within me ly,
        And all things fair
Delighted me that was to be their Heir.

For *Sight* inherits Beauty ; *Hearing*, Sounds ;
      The *Nostril*, sweet Perfumes,
      All Tastes have secret Rooms
Within the *Tongue ;* the *Touching* feeleth Wounds
    Of Pain or Pleasure ; and yet I
Forgat the rest, & was all Sight or Ey,
    Unbody'd & devoid of Care,
Just as in Hev'n the Holy Angels are :
      For simple Sense
Is Lord of all created Excellence.

Being thus prepar'd for all Felicity ;
      Not præpossest with Dross,
      Nor basely glued to gross
And dull Materials that might ruin me,
    Nor fetter'd by an Iron Fate,
By vain Affections in my earthy State,
    To any thing that should seduce
My Sense, or els bereav it of its Use ;
      I was as free
As if there were nor Sin nor Misery.

Pure nativ Powers that Corruption loath,
      Did, like the fairest Glass
      Or spotless polisht Brass,
Themselvs soon in their Object's Image cloath :
    Divine Impressions, when they came,

Did quickly enter & my Soul enflame.
'Tis not the Object, but the Light,
That maketh Hev'n : 'Tis a clearer Sight.
Felicity
Appears to none but them that purely see.

A disentangled & a naked Sense,
A Mind that 's unpossest,
A disengaged Breast,
A quick unprejudic'd Intelligence
Acquainted with the Golden Mean,
An eeven Spirit, quiet, & serene,
Is that where Wisdom's Excellence
And Pleasure keep their Court of Residence.
My Soul get free,
And then thou may'st possess Felicity.

THE APOSTACY

One Star
Is better far
Than many Precious Stones :
One Sun, which is by its own lustre seen,
Is worth ten thousand Golden Thrones :
A juicy Herb, or Spire of Grass,
In useful Virtu, native Green,
An Em'rald doth surpass ;
Hath in 't more Valu, tho less seen.

No Wars,
Nor mortal Jars,
Nor bloody Feuds, nor Coin,
Nor Griefs w^ch *those* occasion, saw I then ;
Nor wicked Thievs w^ch *this* purloin :
I had no Thoughts that were impure ;

Esteeming both Women & Men
God's Work, I was secure,
And reckon'd Peace my choicest Gem.

As *Eve*
I did believ
My self in *Eden* set,
Affecting neither Gold, nor Ermin'd Crowns,
Nor ought els that I need forget ;
No Mud did foul my limpid Streams,
No Mist eclypst my Sun with frowns ;
Set off with hev'nly Beams,
My Joys were Meadows, Fields, & Towns.

Those things
Which *Cherubins*
Did not at first behold
Among God's Works, w^ch *Adam* did not see ;
As Robes, & Stones enchas'd in Gold,
Rich Cabinets, & such like fine
Inventions ; could not ravish me :
I thought not Bowls of Wine
Needful for my Felicity.

All Bliss
Consists in this,
To do as *Adam* did ;
And not to know those superficial Joys
Which were from him in *Eden* hid :
Those little new-invented Things,
Fine Lace & Silks, such Childish Toys
As Ribbans are & Rings,
Or worldly Pelf that Us destroys.

For God,
Both Great & Good,
The Seeds of Melancholy
Creäted not : but only foolish Men,

Grown mad with customary Folly
Which doth increase their Wants, so dote
As when they elder grow they then
    Such Baubles chiefly note ;
More Fools at Twenty Years than Ten.

But I,
    I know not why,
    Did learn among them too
At length ; & where I once with blemisht Eys
    Began their Pence & Toys to view,
    Drown'd in their Customs, I became
    A Stranger to the Shining Skies,
        Lost as a dying Flame ;
    And Hobby-horses brought to prize.

The Sun
    And Moon forgon,
    As if unmade, appear
No more to me ; to God & Heven dead
    I was, as tho they never were. :
    Upon som useless gaudy Book,
    When what I knew of God was fled,
        The Child being taught to look,
    His Soul was quickly murthered.

O fine !
    O most divine !
    O brave ! they cry'd ; & shew'd
Som Tinsel thing whose Glittering did amaze,
    And to their Cries its beauty ow'd ;
    Thus I on Riches, by degrees,
    Of a new Stamp did learn to gaze ;
        While all the World for these
    I lost : my Joy turn'd to a Blaze.

SOLITUDE

How desolate !
Ah ! how forlorn, how sadly did I stand
When in the field my woful State
I felt ! Not all the Land,
Not all the Skies,
Tho Heven shin'd before mine Eys,
Could Comfort yield in any Field to me,
Nor could my Mind Contentment find or see.

Remov'd from Town,
From People, Churches, Feasts, & Holidays,
The Sword of State, the Mayor's Gown,
And all the Neighb'ring Boys ;
As if no Kings
On Earth there were, or living Things,
The silent Skies salute mine Eys, the Seas
My Soul surround ; no Rest I found, or Eas.

My roving Mind
Search'd evry Corner of the spacious Earth,
From Sky to Sky, if it could find,
(But found not) any Mirth :
Not all the Coasts,
Nor all the great & glorious Hosts,
In Hev'n or Earth, did any Mirth afford ;
No welcom Good or needed Food, my Board.

I do believ,
The Ev'ning being shady & obscure,
The very Silence did me griev,
And Sorrow more procure :
A secret Want
Did make me think my Fortune scant.
I was so blind, I could not find my Health,
No Joy mine Ey could there espy, nor Wealth.

Nor could I guess
What kind of thing I long'd for : But that I
    Did somwhat lack of Blessedness,
      Beside the Earth & Sky,
        I plainly found ;
    It griev'd me much, I felt a Wound
Perplex me fore ; yet what my Store should be
I did not know, nothing would shew to me.

        Ye sullen Things !
Ye dumb, ye silent Creatures, & unkind !
    How can I call you Pleasant Springs
      Unless ye eas my Mind !
        Will ye not speak
    What 'tis I want, nor Silence break ?
O pity me, and let me see som Joy ;
Som Kindness shew to me, altho a Boy.

        They silent stood ;
Nor Earth, nor Woods, nor Hills, nor Brooks, nor Skies,
    Would tell me where the hidden Good,
      Which I did long for, lies :
        The shady Trees,
    The Ev'ning dark, the huming Bees,
The chirping Birds, mute Springs & Fords, conspire,
While they deny to answer my Desire.

        Bells ringing I
Far off did hear ; som Country Church they spake ;
    The Noise re-ecchoing throu the Sky
      My Melancholy brake ;
        When 't reacht mine Ear
    Som Tidings thence I hop'd to hear :
But not a Bell me News could tell, or shew
My longing Mind, where Joys to find, or know.

        I griev'd the more,
'Caus I therby somwhat encorag'd was

That I from thence should learn my Store ;
For Churches are a place
That nearer stand
Than any part of all the Land
To Hev'n ; from whence som little Sense I might
To help my Mind receiv, & find som Light.

They louder sound
Than men do talk, somthing they should Disclose ;
The empty Sound did therfore wound
Becaus not shew Repose.
It did revive
To think that Men were there alive ;
But had my Soul, call'd by the Toll, gon in,
I might have found, to eas my Wound, a Thing.

A little Eas
Perhaps, but that might more molest my Mind ;
One flatt'ring Drop would more diseas
My Soul with Thirst, & grind
My Heart with grief :
For Peeple can yield no Relief
In publick sort when in that Court they shine,
Except they mov my Soul with Lov divine.

Th' External Rite,
Altho the face be wondrous sweet & fair,
Can satiate my Appetit
No more than empty Air
Yield solid Food.
Must I the best & highest Good
Seek to possess ; or Blessedness in vain
(Tho 'tis alive in som place) strive to gain ?

O ! what would I
Diseased, wanting, melancholy, giv
To find *that* tru Felicity,
The place where Bliss doth liv ?

Those Regions fair
Which are not lodg'd in Sea nor Air,
Nor Woods, nor Fields, nor Arbour yields, nor Springs,
Nor Hev'ns shew to us below, nor Kings.

I might hav gon
Into the City, Market, Tavern, Street,
Yet only chang'd my Station,
And strove in vain to meet
That Eas of Mind
Which all alone I long'd to find :
A comõn Inn doth no such thing betray,
Nor doth it walk in Peeple's Talk, or Play.

O Eden fair !
Where shall I seek the Soul of Holy Joy
Since I to find it here despair ;
Nor in the shining Day,
Nor in the Shade,
Nor in the Field, nor in a Trade
I can it see ?   Felicity !   Oh, where
Shall I thee find to eas my Mind !   Oh, where !

POVERTY

As in the House I sate
Alone & desolate,
No Creature but the Fire & I,
The Chimney & the Stool, I lift mine Ey
Up to the Wall,
And in the silent Hall
Saw nothing mine
But som few Cups & Dishes shine
The Table & the wooden Stools
Where Peeple us'd to dine :
A painted Cloth there was

Wherin som ancient Story wrought
A little entertain'd my Thought
Which Light discover'd throu the Glass.

I wonder'd much to see
That all my Wealth should be
Confin'd in such a little Room,
Yet hope for more I scarcely durst presume.
It griev'd me sore
That such a scanty Store
Should be my All :
For I forgat my Eas & Health,
Nor did I think of Hands or Eys,
Nor Soul nor Body prize ;
I neither thought the Sun,
Nor Moon, nor Stars, nor Peeple, *mine,*
Tho they did round about me shine ;
And therfore was I quite undon.

Som greater things I thought
Must needs for me be wrought,
Which till my craving Mind could see
I ever should lament my Poverty :
I fain would have
Whatever Bounty gave ;
Nor could there be
Without, or Lov or Deity :
For, should not He be Infinit
Whose Hand created me ?
Ten thousand absent things
Did vex my poor & wanting Mind,
Which, till I be no longer blind,
Let me not see the King of Kings.

His Lov must surely be
Rich, infinit, & free ;
Nor can He be thought a God
Of Grace & Pow'r, that fills not his Abode,

His Holy Court,
In kind & liberal Sort ;
Joys & Pleasures,
Plenty of Jewels, Goods, & Treasures,
(To enrich the Poor, cheer the forlorn)
His Palace must adorn,
And given all to me :
For till *His* Works *my* Wealth became,
No Lov, or Peace, did me enflame :
But now I have a DEITY.

CHRISTENDOM

WHEN first mine Infant-Ear
Of *Christendom* did hear,
I much admir'd what kind of Place or Thing
It was of which the Folk did talk :
What Coast, what Region, what therin
Did mov, or might be seen to walk.
My great Desire
Like ardent fire
Did long to know what Things did ly behind
That *Mystic Name*, to wch mine Ey was blind.

Som Depth it did conceal,
Which till it did reveal
Its self to me, no Quiet, Peace, or Rest,
Could I by any Means attain ;
My earnest Thoughts did me molest
Till som one should the thing explain :
I thought it was
A Glorious Place,
Where Souls might dwell in all Delight & Bliss ;
So thought, yet fear'd that I the Truth might miss :

Among ten thousand things,
Gold, Silver, Cherub's Wings,

Pearls, Rubies, Diamonds, a Church wth Spires,
  Masks, Stages, Games & Plays,
  That then might suit my yong Desires,
  Feathers. & Farthings, Holidays,
      Cards, Musick, Dice,
      So much in price ;
A *City* did before mine Eys present
Its self, wherin there reigned sweet Content.

    A Town beyond the Seas,
      Whose Prospect much did pleas,
And to my Soul so sweetly raise Delight
  As if a long expected Joy,
  Shut up in that transforming Sight,
  Would into me its Self convey ;
      And Blessedness
      I there possess,
As if that City stood on my own Ground,
And all the Profit mine wch there was found.

    Whatever Force me led,
      My Spirit sweetly fed
On these Conceits ; That 'twas a City strange,
  Wherin I saw no gallant Inns,
  No Markets, New or Old Exchange,
  No Childish Trifles, useless Things ;
      Nor any Bound
      That Town surround ;
But as if all its Streets ev'n endless were ;
Without or Gate or Wall it did appear.

    Things Native sweetly grew,
      Which there mine Ey did view,
Plain, simple, cheap, on either side the Street,
  Which was exceeding fair & wide ;
  Sweet Mansions there mine Eys did meet ;
  Green Trees the shaded Doors did hide :

My chiefest Joys
Were Girls & Boys
That in those Streets still up & down did play,
Which crown'd the Town with constant Holiday.

A sprightly pleasant Time,
(Ev'n Summer in its prime)
Did gild the Trees, the Houses, Children, Skies,
And made the City all divine ;
It ravished my wondring Eys
To see the Sun so brightly shine :
The Heat & Light
Seem'd in my sight
With such a dazling Lustre shed on them,
As made me think 'twas th' *New Jerusalem.*

Beneath the lofty Trees
I saw, of all Degrees,
Folk calmly sitting in their doors ; while som
Did standing with them kindly talk,
Som smile, som sing, or what was don
Observ, while others by did walk ;
They view'd the Boys
And Girls, their Joys,
The Streets adorning with their Angel-faces,
Themselvs diverting in those pleasant Places.

The Streets like Lanes did seem,
Not pav'd with Stones, but green,
Which with red Clay did partly mixt appear ;
'Twas Holy Ground of great Esteem ;
The Springs choice Liveries did wear
Of verdant Grass that grew between
The purling Streams,
Which golden Beams
Of Light did varnish, coming from the Sun,
By wch to distant Realms was Service don.

In fresh & cooler Rooms
Retir'd they dine : Perfumes
They wanted not, having the pleasant Shade,
  And Peace to bless their House within,
  By sprinkled Waters cooler made,
  For those incarnat Cherubin.
      This happy Place,
      With all the Grace
The Joy & Beauty which did it beseem,
Did ravish me & highten my Esteem.

    That here to rais Desire
    All Objects do conspire,
Peeple in Years, & Yong enough to play,
  Their Streets of Houses, comõn Peace,
  In one continued Holy day
  Whose gladsom Mirth shall never cease :
      Since these becom
      My *Christendom,*
What learn I more than that *Jerusalem*
Is *mine,* as 'tis *my Maker's,* choicest Gem.

    Before I was aware
    Truth did to me appear,
And represented to my Virgin-Eys
  Th' unthought of Joys & Treasures
  Wherin my Bliss & Glory lies ;
  My God's Delight, (wch givs me Measure)
      His Turtle Dov,
      Is Peace & Lov
In Towns : for holy Children, Maids, & Men
Make up the King of Glory's Diadem.

NATURE

THAT *Custom* is a Second *Nature,* we
Most plainly find by Nature's Purity :

For Nature teacheth nothing but the Truth ;
I'm sure *mine* did so, in my Virgin-Youth.
As soon as He my Spirit did inspire,
His Works He bid me in the World admire
My Senses were Informers of my Heart,
The Conduits of His Glory, Pow'r, & Art :
His Greatness, Wisdom, Goodness, I did see,
Endearing Lov, & vast Eternity,
Almost as soon as born ; & ev'ry Sense
Was in me like to som Intelligence.
I was by nature prone & apt to lov
All Light & Beauty, both in Hev'n abov
And Earth beneath ; was ready to admire,
Adore & prais, as well as to desire.
My Inclinations rais'd me up on high,
And guided me to trace Infinity.
A secret Self I had enclos'd within,
That was not bounded with my Cloaths or Skin,
Or terminated with my Sight, whose Sphere
Ran parallel with that of Heven here :
And did, much like the subtil piercing Light,
When fenc'd from rough & boistrous Storms by night,
Break throu the Lanthorn-sides, & with its Ray
Diffuse its Glory spreading evry way :
Whose steddy Beams, too subtil for the Wind,
Are such that we their Bounds can hardly find.
It did encompass & possess Rare Things,
But yet felt more ; & on Angelick Wings
Pierc'd throu the Skies imediatly, & sought
For all that could beyond all Worlds be thought.
It did not go or mov, but in me stood,
And by dilating of its self, all Good
It try'd to reach ; I found it present there,
Ev'n while it did remain conversing here ;
And more suggested than I could discern,
Or ever since by any means could learn.
Vast, unaffected, wonderful, Desires,
Like nativ, ardent, inward, hidden Fires,

Sprang up, with Expectations very strange,
Which into stronger Hopes did quickly change ;
For all I saw beyond the Azure Round
Seem'd endless Darkness, with no Beauty crown'd.
Why Light should not be there as well as here ;
Why Goodness should not likewise there appear ;
Why Treasures & Delights should bounded be
Since there is such a wide Infinity :
These were the Doubts & Troubles of my Soul,
By wch we may perceiv (without controul)
A World of endless Joys by Nature made
That needs must always flourish, never fade.
A wide, magnificent, & spacious Sky,
A Fabrick worthy of the Deity ;
Clouds here & there like winged Chariots flying.
Flowers ever flourishing, yet always dying ;
A Day of Glory where I all things see
Enricht with Beams of Light as 'twere for me
And that, after the Sun withdraws his Light,
Succeeded with a shady glorious Night ;
The Moon & Stars shedding their Influence
On all things, as appears to common Sense :
With secret Rooms in Times & Ages more
Past & to com, enlarging my great Store.
These all in Order present unto me
My happy Eys were able then to see,
With other Wonders, to my Soul unknown
Till they by Men & Reading first were shewn.
And yet there were many new Regions more
Into all which my new-fledg'd Soul did soar,
Whose endless Spaces, like a Cabinet,
Were fill'd with various Joys in order set.
The *Empty*, like to wide & vacant Room
For Fancy to enlarge in, & presume
A Space for more, not fathom'd yet, implies
The Boundlessness of what I ought to prize.
Here I was seated to behold New Things
In th' August-Mansion of the King of Kings ;

And All was *mine*.   The Author yet not known,
But that there must be one was plainly shewn ;
Which Fountain of Delights must needs *be Lov*
As all the Goodness of the Things did prov :
Of whose Enjoiment I am made the End,
While, how the same is so, I comprehend.

DUMNESS

SURE Man was born to meditat on things,
And to contemplat the Eternal Springs
Of God & Nature, Glory, Bliss, & Pleasure ;
That Life & Lov might be his chiefest Treasure :
And therfore *Speechless* made at first, that he
Might in himself profoundly busied be ;
Not giving vent before he hath ta'n in
Such Antidotes as guard his Soul from Sin.
　Wise Nature made him *Deaf* too, that he might
Not be disturb'd while he doth take Delight
In inward Things ; not be deprav'd with Tongues,
Nor injur'd by the Errors & the Wrongs
That *mortal Words* convey : For Sin & Death
Are most infused by accursed Breath
That, flowing from corrupted Intrails, bear
Those hidden Plagues wch Souls may justly fear.
　This, (my dear Friends) this was my blessed Case ;
For, nothing spake to me but the fair Face
Of Hev'n & Earth, when yet I could not speak :
I did my Bliss, when I did Silence, break.
My Non-Intelligence of Human Words
Ten thousand Pleasures unto me affords :
For, while I knew not what to me they said ;
Before *Their* Souls were into *Mine* convey'd ;
Before *that* Living Vehicle of Wind
Did breathe into me their infected Mind ;
Before My Thoughts with Theirs were levened,
The Gate of Souls as yet not opened :

Then did I dwell within a World of Light
Retir'd & separat from all mens Sight ;
Where I did feel strange Thoughts, & Secrets see
That were (or seem'd) only reveal'd to Me :
There I saw all the World enjoy'd by Me ;
There All Things seem'd to end in Me alone :
No Business serious deem'd, but that wch is
Design'd to perfect my Eternal Bliss.

    D'ye ask me What ?   It was for to admire
The Satisfaction of all Just Desire :
'Twas to be pleas'd with all that God had don :
'Twas to enjoy All that's beneath the Sun :
'Twas with a steddy, quick, & lively Sense
Duly to estimat the Excellence
Of all God's Works : T' inherit endless Treasure
And to be fill'd with Everlasting Pleasure :
To prize, & prais.   Thus was I shut within
A Fort impregnable to any Sin,
Till the Avenues being open laid,
Whole Legions enter'd, & the Fort betray'd.

    Yer * which unhappy time, within my Mind
A Temple & a Teacher I could find,
With a large Text to com̄ent on : No Ear,
But Eys themselvs were all the Hearers there ;
And evry Stone & evry Star a Tongue,
And evry Gale of Wind a Psalm or Song :
The Hevens were an Oracle, & spake
Divinity ; the Earth did undertake
The Office of a Priest ; and I b'ing dumb,
(Nothing besides was so) All things did com
With Voices & Instructions. But when I
Had learnt to speak, their Pow'r began to dy :
Mine Ears let other Noises in, not theirs ;
A Noise disturbing all my Hymns & Pray'rs :
My Foes pull'd down my Temple to the ground,
And my untainted Soul did deeply wound ;
Marr'd all my inward Faculties ; destroy'd

* Yer=ere.

The Oracle, & all I there enjoy'd.
  Yet to mine Infancy what first appear'd ;
Those Truths w^{ch} (being Speechless) I had heard,
Preventing all the rest, got such a Root
Within my Heart, & stick to close unto't ;
It may be trampled on ; but still will grow,
And Nutriment to *Soil* its self will ow.
The first Impressions are immortal all :
And let my Foes cry ne'r so loud, or call ;
Yet these still whisper, if I will but hear,
And penetrat the Heart, if not the Ear.

SILENCE

A QUIET silent Person may possess
All that is Great or Good in Blessedness :
The Inward Work is the Supream ; for all
The other were occasion'd by the Fall.
A man, that seemeth Idle to the view
Of others, may the greatest Business do :
Those Acts which *Adam* in his Innocence
Was to perform, had all the Excellence :
Others which he knew not (how good fo-e'r)
Are meaner Matters, of a lower Sphere ;
Building of Churches ; Giving to the Poor ;
In Dust & Ashes lying on the floor ;
Administring of Justice ; Preaching Peace ;
Plowing & Toiling for a forc'd Increas ;
With Visiting the Sick, or Governing
The Rude & Ignorant. This was a thing
As then unknown : for neither Ignorance,
Nor Poverty, nor Sickness, did advance
Their Banner in the World, till Sin came in ;
Since *that*, *these* to be needful did begin.
  The first & only Work he had to do,
Was, of his Bliss to take a grateful View ;
In all the Goods he did possess, rejoice ;

Sing Praises to his God with cheerful voice ;
T' express his hearty Thanks, & inward Lov,
Which is the best accepted Work abov
Them all.   And this at first was *mine :* These were
My Exercises of the highest Sphere.
To see, approv, take pleasure, & rejoice
In Heart ; is better than the loudest Nois.
No Melody in Words can equal *that :*
The sweetest Organ, Lute, or Harp, is flat
And dull, compar'd therto.   O ! that I still
Could prize my Father's Lov & Holy Will !
This is to honor, worship, & adore ;
This is to fear Him ; nay, it is far more :
'Tis to enjoy him, & to imitate
The very Life & Bliss of His High 'State :
'Tis to receiv with holy Reverence
His mighty Gifts, & with a fitting Sense
Of pure Devotion, & Humility,
To prize his Works, his Lov to magnify.
  O happy Ignorance of other Things,
Which made me present with the King of Kings,
And like Him too !   All Spirit, Life, & Power,
Wreathed into a never-fading Bower.
A World of Innocence as then was mine,
In which the Joys of Paradise did shine ;
And while I was not here, I was in Heven,
Not Resting *One*, but evry Day, in *Seven :*
At all times minding with a lively Sense
The Univers in all its Excellence.
No other Thoughts did intervene, to cloy,
Divert, extinguish, or eclyps my Joy :
No Worldly Customs, new-found Wants or Dreams
Invented here, polluted my pure Streams :
No Wormwood-Star into my Sea did fall ;
No rotten Seed, or Bitterness of Gall,
Tainted my Soul.   From all Contagion free,
I could discern with an unclouded Ey,
In that fair World One onely was the Friend,

One Spring, one living Stream, one only End ;
There only One did sacrifise & sing
To only One Eternal Hev'nly King :
The Union was so strict betwixt the Two,
That All was Either's which my Soul did view ;
His Gifts, & my Possessions, both our Treasures ;
He *Mine*, & I the Ocean of *His* Pleasures :
He was an Ocean of Delights, from whom
The Springs of Life & Streams of Bliss did com ;
My Bosom was an Ocean into which
They all did run, that me they might enrich.
A vast & measure-less Capacity
Enlarg'd my Soul like to the Deity,
In whose mysterious Mind & potent Hand
All Ages & all Worlds together stand ;
Who, tho He nothing *said*, did always reign,
And in Himself *Eternity* contain.
When in my Soul the King of Kings did fit,
The World was more *in me*, than I *in it*.
And to Himself, in Me, He ever gave
All that He takes Delight to see me have.
Ev'n thus my Spirit was an Endless Sphere,
Like God himself ; He, Hev'n, & Earth, being there.

ON LEAPING OVER THE MOON

I saw new Worlds beneath the Water ly,
    New Peeple ; yea, another Sky
        And Sun, which seen by Day
        Might things more clear display.
            Just such another
            Of late my Brother
Did in his Travel see, & saw by Night,
    A much more strange & wondrous Sight :
Nor could the World exhibit such another,
    So Great a Sight, but in a Brother.

Adventure strange ! No such in Story we
  New or old, tru or feigned, see.
     On Earth he seem'd to mov
    Yet Heven went abov ;
       Up in the Skies
       His Body flies
In open, visible, yet *Magick*, fort :
  As he along the Way did sport,
Over the Flood he takes his nimble Cours
  Without the help of feigned Horse.

As he went tripping o'r the King's high-way,
  A little pearly River lay
     O'r which, without a Wing
    Or Oar, he dar'd to swim,
      Swim throu the Air
      On Body fair ;
He would not use nor trust *Icarian* Wings
  Lest they should prov deceitful things ;
For had he faln, it had been wondrous high,
  Not from, but from abov, the Sky :

He might hav dropt throu that thin Element
  Into a fathomless Descent ;
     Unto the nether Sky
    That did beneath him ly,
      And there might tell
      What Wonders dwell
On Earth abov.   Yet doth he briskly run,
  And bold the Danger overcom ;
Who, as he leapt, with Joy related soon
  How *happy he* o'r-leapt the Moon.

What wondrous things upon the Earth are don
  Beneath, & yet abov, the Sun ?
     Deeds all appear again
    In higher Spheres ; remain
      In Clouds as yet :

But there they get
Another Light, & in another way
 Themselvs to us *abov* display.
The Skies themselvs this earthly Globe surround ;
 W' are even here within them found.

On hev'nly Ground within the Skies we walk,
 And in this middle Center talk :.
  Did we but wisely mov,
  On Earth in Hev'n abov,
   Then soon should we
   Exalted be
Abov the Sky : from whence whoever falls,
 Through a long dismall Precipice,
Sinks to the deep Abyss where *Satan* crawls
 Where horrid Death & Despair lies.

As much as others thought themselvs to ly
 Beneath the Moon, so much more high
  Himself he thought to fly
  Abov the starry Sky,
   As *that* he spy'd
   Below the Tide.
Thus did he yield me in the shady Night
 A wondrous & instructiv Light,
Which taught me that under our Feet there is,
 As o'r our Heads, a Place of Bliss.

To the same purpos ; he, not long before
 Brought home from Nurse, going to the door
  To do som little thing
  He must not do within,
   With Wonder cries,
   As in the Skies
He saw the Moon, *O yonder is the Moon*
 Newly com after me to Town,
That shin'd at Lugwardin but yesternight,
 Where I enjoy'd the self-same Light.

As if it had ev'n twenty thousand faces,
    It shines at once in many places ;
        To all the Earth so wide
        God doth the Stars divide
          With so much Art
          The Moon impart,
They serv us all ; serv wholy ev'ry One
    As if they served him alone.
While evry single Person hath such Store,
    'Tis want of Sense that makes us poor.

THE REVIEW

    MY Child-hood is a Sphere
Wherin ten thousand hev'nly Joys appear :
      Those *Thoughts* it doth include,
    And those Affections, which review'd,
      Again present to me
In better sort the *Things* that I did see,
    Imaginations *Reall* are,
    Unto my Mind again repair :
Which makes my Life a Circle of Delights ;
A hidden Sphere of obvious Benefits :
An Earnest that the Actions of the Just
Shall still revive, & flourish in the Dust.

Printed in Great Britain by
Thomas Nelson and Sons Ltd, Edinburgh